D1378543

THE CRUSADES

THE CRUSADES

HOLY WAR, PIETY AND POLITICS IN CHRISTENDOM FROM THE FIRST CRUSADE TO THE RECONQUISTA

CHRIS McNAB

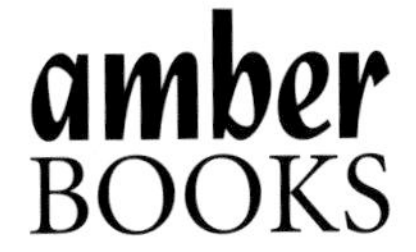

This Amber Books edition published in 2019

Published by
Amber Books Ltd
United House
North Road
London
N7 9DP
United Kingdom
www.amberbooks.co.uk
Instagram: amberbooksltd
Facebook: www.facebook.com/amberbooks
Twitter: @amberbooks
Pinterest: amberbooksltd

Project Editor: Michael Spilling
Designer: Zoe Mellors
Picture Research: Terry Forshaw

ISBN: 978-1-78274-900-4

Printed in China

Contents

ceut les messaiges & les prie moult debona
irement & quant ilz orent demoure a sa cou
rt tant comme il leur pleut Il les fist convoier
& leur donna de ses richesses . Cy fine le
premier livre le victorich charlemaine .

Ci comence le second livre des histoires char
lemaine / premierement coment il fut cou
ronne a empereur en leglise saint pierre
de Romme / Apres coment il condampna

Introduction: A Climate for Crusading

The Crusades began in the late eleventh century, in a blaze of religious fervour, but their historical roots twisted far further back through time. Indeed, it took centuries of religious, military and imperial turmoil to produce the First Crusade, and thereafter further centuries for the Crusades to play out to their conclusion.

Any study of the Crusades must carefully negotiate a world of potential pitfalls, traps for the historically unwary. The Crusades, despite being centuries distant from our own time, form one of those periods of history that continues to pulse with political and ideological undercurrents. Some argue that the modern tensions between a 'Christian' West (the religious adjective is rather nominal in the modern context) and an Islamic East can in many ways be charted directly back to the Crusades, the cruel wars between the faiths establishing deep roots of antagonism, and forming spiritual and geopolitical fault lines that refuse to disappear.

Opposite: The coronation of Charlemagne as Emperor of the West by Pope Leo III in Rome on Christmas Day, 800.

Yet as with so much of history, interpretation is everything. Today the very term 'Crusades' is not so much an historical definition, but rather a gladiatorial ring in which various contrasting arguments and perceptions slug it out. Attempting a neutral definition, we can say that the Crusades was a series of religious wars from the late eleventh century to the end of the thirteenth century (although some extend them as late as the sixteenth century). They were principally, though far from exclusively, characterized by conflicts between Christian and Muslim armies for control of territory in the Middle East, especially what we today term the 'Holy Land', with deep religious significance for both faiths. In total there were nine Crusades dotted throughout our period, although the first four were certainly the most significant, and will therefore take the lion's share of our analysis.

For some, the Crusades implies a romantically outdated time of religious idealism, the Christian West responding to what it saw as a clear and present danger to its values and heritage.

Below: The crusader commander Godfrey of Bouillon directs his soldiers in an assault against a Muslim fortress during the First Crusade.

Others see them, by contrast, as naked imperial aggression, attempted land grabs by empires cruelly disdainful of local cultures. Many shades of opinion exist between these two poles. As this book will show, however, simple 'us vs them' arguments, seen from either side of the wars, break down considerably when subjected to more cautious evaluation. For the Crusades were an irreducibly complex period of history, replete with contradictions and unexpected shifts. For example, peaceful (or at least pragmatic) negotiated coexistence between Christians and Muslims was as much a feature of the Crusading period as brutal conflict. Even militarily, the divisions could be blurred; on occasions, Christian and Muslim armies fought side by side against other mixed-faith forces. Frequently, Christians fought Christians and Muslims fought Muslims – neither side was either uniform nor united, each split by tribal, regional or political interests, and pulled in often unexpected directions by mercurial leaders.

Above: As a crusade leader, Bishop Adémar of Puy demonstrated how spiritual office and warrior skills could exist comfortably side by side, even in a Church official.

In this book, we will present both the fundamentals and the complexities of this astonishing time in international history. It is a story of great highs – both exceptional courage and high culture abound – and the most hideous lows, usually in the form of atrocities of such magnitude and depravity that they still command the power to shock. Our story begins, however, with seeds of conflict sown many years before the first crusaders set out for the Holy Land.

Right: Crusaders fighting against the Muslims in c. 1185. The scene of beheadings on the left illustrates how piety was frequently matched or exceeded by brutality.

EMPIRES AND FAITHS

Setting the context for the Crusades requires an understanding of the various strategic, religious and political interests that dominated Europe, the Balkans, the Middle East, North Africa and Central Asia from the sixth to the eleventh centuries. A certain degree of simplification is required here, as, like much history from the imperial ages, the story is often one of fiendish complexity. Ambition was naked, sly and opportunistic in this era, and when combined with labyrinthine dynastic relations and constant shifts in power and economy, resulted in a world of ever-shifting allegiances and oppositions. The first step to understanding the Crusades, however, is to map out the key power blocs and the often brittle relations between them.

The Byzantine Empire

At its height, at the beginning of the second century AD, the Roman Empire stretched from Britain in the west to Mesopotamia in the east. Yet between the third and fifth centuries, the western part of the empire underwent a progressive collapse under the depredations of barbarian tribes, culminating with the death of the last Western Roman emperor, Flavius

Julius Nepos, in 480. The eastern parts of the empire managed to survive, however, and were consolidated under the eastern imperial court first established by Emperor Diocletian (r. 284–305) and boosted by Emperor Constantine (r. 306–37). Not only did Constantine adopt Christianity as the official state religion, he also centred the Roman Empire on a new capital, the city of Byzantium, in 330, renaming it Constantinople. By 600, this city (present-day Istanbul in Turkey), having risen to a state of unrivalled wealth and opulence, presided over what we know as the Byzantine Empire, which included parts of southern Spain and strips of central, northern and southern Italy, the islands of Sicily, Sardinia and Corsica, the Balkans and Anatolia (present-day Turkey), much of the eastern Mediterranean, including Palestine, plus Egypt and large parts of North Africa.

Below: The Roman Emperor Diocletian brought about the administrative partition of the Roman Empire into Eastern and Western parts.

The Christianization of the Eastern Roman Empire had numerous ethnic, social and political consequences, not least the ascendancy of the city of Jerusalem. Emperor Constantine appointed his mother, Helena, as *Augusta Imperatrix*, and gave her the authority and financial means to reconstruct Palestine's holy places as spiritual centres of Christendom. This had a transformative effect on Jerusalem, including the construction of the Church of the Holy Sepulchre in 330, upon the purported site of Christ's crucifixion. Jerusalem, and other holy sites in Palestine, thereafter became magnetic destinations for pilgrimage from across the Christian world, a tradition that would continue into the Middle Ages and would eventually become militarized during the Crusades.

As we shall see, the Byzantine Empire was a frequently fractured and imperilled entity, the territorial extent of the empire contracting and expanding over time. Threats to Byzantium were both internal – the empire was riven by domestic and regional factions – and external, with outside aggressors including the Normans, Franks, pagan tribes of Northern Europe and, eventually, the rapid growth of the Islamic world. There was also a religious tension between the Eastern Empire's Greek-centred Orthodox Christianity and the Latin Catholic Christianity controlled by the papacy in Western Europe; a shared spiritual root would not prevent a pervasive suspicion and even outright hostility governing relations between these two centres of Christianity. Despite this friction, the Byzantine Empire was, even for the papacy, a Christian bulwark against the intrusion of various non-Christian beliefs from the Middle East and Asia.

The Holy Roman Empire

The bulk of the participants in what we call the First Crusade (1096–99) were Franks, a people of Germanic origin who emerged in the third century but whose monarchs, during the Middle Ages, came to rule over much of Western Europe, thereby widening the umbrella of the Franks to many territories beyond their Germanic homelands. A critical event in the history of Frankish people was the crowning of their king Charlemagne (r. 800–14) as emperor in 800 by Pope Leo III. This act of coronation, which took place in St Peter's Basilica in Rome, resurrected the imperial title in Western Europe, with the full blessing of the Church, and theoretically gave Charlemagne secular authority over most of the rulers of Europe. Charlemagne died in 814, opening the floodgates for imperial infighting that fragmented his empire, which roughly came to be split between modern-day Germany and France. The German Empire, however, became known as the Holy Roman Empire, a title that would endure until the nineteenth century.

A CRITICAL EVENT IN THE HISTORY OF FRANKISH PEOPLE WAS THE CROWNING OF THEIR KING CHARLEMAGNE (R. 800–14) AS EMPEROR IN 800.

Relations between the papacy and the Holy Roman Empire would, as we shall see, be subject to breakdown. Yet the papacy's key role in the founding of this empire, meant that when the time came to form a crusading army, it could appeal directly to an imperial machinery to maximize its manpower, political influence and financial muscle.

Before moving on to consider the papacy directly, we must mention another influential people in Europe – the Normans. These warrior-like folk, centred in northern France, were of mixed ethnic background, a tenth-century fusion of Norse Viking, Frankish and Gallo-Roman blood. As much as the Normans were known for their cultural advances, particularly in fields such as architecture and music, they were also rightfully feared for their military prowess. The most famous of the Norman conquests was that of England in 1066, secured by William the Conqueror's victory at the battle of Hastings. The Normans would also exert a peripheral influence over the history of the Crusades, both for their attacks upon Byzantine territories, especially those in Italy, and for their participation in the Crusades and the establishment of some of the crusader states. The ambiguous status of the Normans in relation to the objectives of the Crusades should not, however, necessarily be seen as vacillating or confused – the Middle Ages were a time of ever-shifting loyalties, with each player in the drama constantly seeking ways to take centre stage.

Below: A medieval representation of St Peter. In the Western Church he was regarded as the founding Pope, while in the Eastern Church he was the first Patriarch of Antioch.

The papacy

The papacy of the Roman Catholic Church tracked and proclaimed its authority all the way back to the establishment of the Christian church by St Peter. (According to Catholic doctrine, St Peter was the founding head of the church, from which all subsequent Popes have been divinely appointed successors.) Papal influence was weak until the Christianization of the Roman Empire under Constantine. Even then, from its headquarters in Rome, the Church struggled for authority with the wider world, with varying degrees of success, clashing particularly with the leaders of the Holy Roman Empire and the Byzantine Empire. Summarizing greatly, the papacy's chief objective was to extend its spiritual leadership over temporal rulers, i.e. the kings and queens of Europe, plus assert its own brand of Christianity against emerging or established alternatives.

Above: A dark vision of the destruction of Rome by the Normans in 1084 by the forces of Emperor Henry IV; the Normans torched the city to quash Roman resistance.

In relation to the Crusades, one of the seminal events in the history of the papacy was the 'Great Schism' of 1054, in which a series of doctrinal differences led to a split between the Greek Eastern Church and the Latin Western Church, the rival centres of Christianity now divided between Constantinople and Rome. Although the First Crusade, launched just over 40 years later, ostensibly showed solidarity between the Greek and Latin churches, we should always be mindful of the theological rivalry in play, which could influence both military and strategic decisions.

The Great Schism took place during an important period of reform in the Church. For all its trappings of piety, by c. 1040 the reputation of the Latin Church had become somewhat sullied by corruption, violence, political manoeuvring and the frequently sordid misbehaviour of its representatives, both high and low. As a backlash, there thus began a reformist movement, focused upon restoring the Church's ethical purity – especially through improved standards of education and behaviour among the clergy and widespread church-building – and also on regaining the Church's authority over Europe's lords and kings. A central figure in the reformist movement was Pope Gregory VII, who took the papacy in 1073. Gregory brought rigour to reform, diligently enforcing the rules of celibacy among the clergy and quashing the practice of simony (the selling of church offices and positions).

The latter contributed to what became known as the Investiture Controversy, the rather legalistic title not doing full justice to the importance of this event in European history. Prior to 1075, the Holy Roman Emperor had claimed sole authority to appoint Popes; extending the principle, bishops and abbots were therefore appointed by members of the senior nobility. It was a situation ripe for corruption, as nobles often appointed themselves or their children to the Church positions, mindful of the extensive wealth and land holdings that frequently came with ordination. The push-back against this situation began even before Gregory's time, when in 1059 a Church council in Rome reclaimed the right to appoint the Pope, acting on the fact that the German king, Henry IV, was only six years old at the time. Gregory consolidated Church power over investiture with his *Dictatus Papae* in 1075, by which time Henry IV had come of age. The German king reacted aggressively, declaring his right of investiture and calling for the election of a new Pope. Matters escalated over subsequent years, and peaked in 1080 when Henry unilaterally appointed a new Pope (Antipope Clement III) and then, the following year, actually invaded Rome, intending to take direct control of the papacy. Gregory called up his allies, particularly the Normans and various Italian states. The Normans ultimately defeated the Germans, but sacked Rome in the process and caused Gregory to flee as Rome's citizens rebelled against him.

NOBLES OFTEN APPOINTED THEMSELVES OR THEIR CHILDREN TO THE CHURCH POSITIONS, MINDFUL OF THE EXTENSIVE WEALTH AND LAND HOLDINGS THAT FREQUENTLY CAME WITH ORDINATION.

The Investiture Crisis rumbled on for two decades more, causing factional violence both in Italy and within the German Empire. Gregory died in 1085, but steadily the papacy gained the upper hand in the struggle. It made a measure of peace with the Byzantine emperor Alexios I (r. 1081–1118), who had at first actually given financial support to Henry for his military campaigns; Henry's power was weakened by the rapprochement. The Normans, bolstered by the Church's offer of spiritual rewards for earthly service, gained the upper hand over the imperial forces in Germany. Furthermore, Pope Urban II (in office from 1088 to 1099) cleverly built up support for his office and his reforms in wider Europe, such that by the time of the First Crusade the Investiture Controversy had largely been settled in favour of the Church.

Below: A map of Muslim Jerusalem. The area inside the wall includes some of the holiest sites of Christendom, Islam and Judaism.

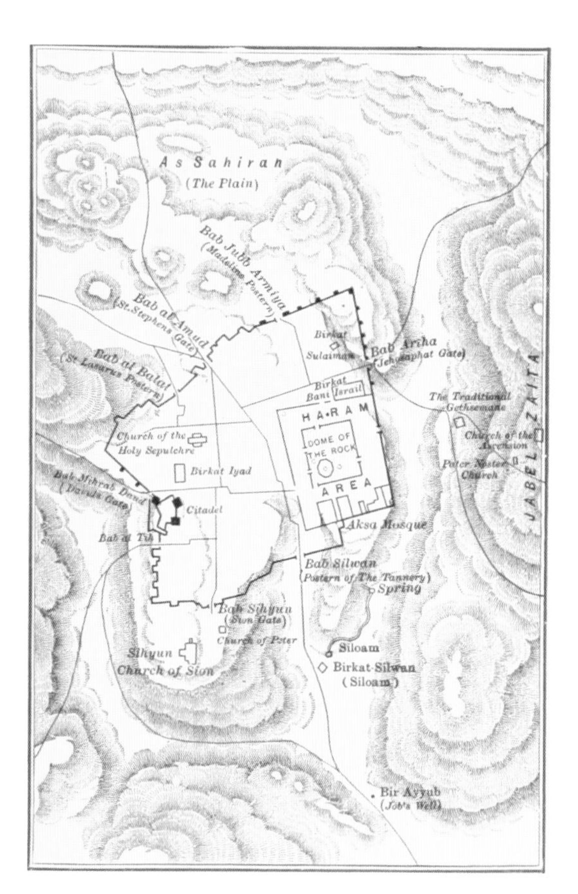

The Muslim Empire

The term 'Muslim Empire' is admittedly crude, used merely to invoke the extent of Islamic conquest and influence between the seventh century and the end of the Crusades. For in much the same way as the various European or Byzantine empires, the world of the Muslims was not a single entity. Instead it was divided between both contrasting theological interpretations and the ambitions of various warlords and rulers, which often resulted in as much inter-Muslim violence as it did military campaigning against the crusaders. What cannot be denied, however, was the sheer force and dynamism with which Islam exploded onto the world stage.

The birth of Islam began in AD 610 in a remote cave above the town of Mecca in Arabia. There the Prophet Muhammad, a 40-year-old merchant, received the revelations of God via the angel Gabriel. With extraordinary speed, these revelations, channelled through extraordinary missionary zeal, spread the religion of Islam far and wide, quickly bursting out from Mecca and Medina (the places in which Muhammad initially preached) and within just two decades becoming the dominant religion of the Arabian Peninsula.

WAR AND FAITH IN MEDIEVAL CHRISTIANITY

Left: The Devil presents St Augustine with the Book of Vices. Medieval morality was a constant struggle between good and evil.

THE MIDDLE AGES IS a complex landscape of beliefs and practices. Certainly, matters of religious faith – and the interpretation of that faith – held universal sway in Europe. During the 1960s and 1970s, it became common for revisionist historians to regard Western Christianity almost as a front for naked imperialism. Yet alongside appalling violence, piety, or at least the attempt to achieve it, seemed to be genuine among many, even those who lived most rapaciously by the sword. The warriors who signed up to the Crusades did so in awareness that their commitment would result in terrible hardship (for both themselves and their families), uncertain outcomes and possibly death, but still remained motivated by the expiation of sins promised for their participation in a *praelia sancta* (holy war). Fear of hell, concern over purgatory and a yearning to achieve salvation were deep-seated convictions in medieval Christian society (there was almost no countervailing viewpoint), so any act that brought full *indulgence* (complete forgiveness for sins, enabling a person to pass straight to heaven upon death) was highly attractive. Furthermore, medieval rulers could draw upon long-established theological justifications for armed conflict, doctrines that bypassed some of Christianity's more pacifistic leanings. In the fifth century, the great St Augustine had laid down the conditions of the 'just war', arguing that if war was made by a rightfully appointed authority, using minimum violence and principally in the cause of self-defence or defence of others, it could be declared right in the eyes of God. This foundation was spun in all manner of ways in succeeding centuries, meaning that by the time of the Crusades conflict and Christianity had been largely reconciled. Yet there was enough self-inspection in medieval theology for many people to question crusading on religious grounds. One Sigebert of Gembloux, a contemporary Benedictine monk (and admittedly a supporter of the imperial powers during the Investiture Controversy), argued that Urban II's call to arms for the First Crusade was essentially a sly attempt to convert a *militia mundi* (army of the world) into a *militia Dei* (army of God).

THREE SPHERES OF ISLAM

In its broadest outlines, historical Islam divided the world into three main spheres of belief:

***Dar al-Islam* – lit. 'House of Islam'. This term refers to those countries in which Islam is the dominant religion, both in the general population and in the governing administration. Those Muslims who therefore live within the *Dar al-Islam* are free to practice their religion without restriction or repression.**

***Dar al-Harb* – lit. 'House of War'. *Dar al-Harb* indicated non-Islamic countries that did not have treaties of peace or non-aggression with neighbouring or nearby Islamic states. A state of conflict is therefore potential or actual between the *Dar al-Islam* and the *Dar al-Harb*.**

***Dar al-'Ahd* – lit. 'House of Truce'. This refers to non-Muslim states, those who had agreed peace treaties or pacts of non-aggression with Muslim nations. This type of arrangement was extremely important even during the time of the Crusades, as for both Muslim and non-Muslim states a continual state of war was largely regarded as undesirable.**

Islam could not contain itself within such a limited area, however, and the faith tied itself to military expansion into the wider Middle East, taking the spiritual dimension of *jihad* ('holy war', specifically within oneself) and applying it to war against non-believers, or some of them at least. The rate at which the Muslim world expanded was astonishing, and largely conducted at the expense of the Persian and Byzantine Empires. By 750, less than 150 years after Muhammad received his revelation, Islamic armies had not only conquered Arabia, but also Syria and the Levant, most of the Persian Empire (including what is today Iran and Iraq), northern India, North Africa (from Egypt to what is today northern Morocco), plus the Iberian Peninsula, the latter bringing the Islamic conquest directly into Western Europe.

It was an astonishing feat of arms and faith, and one that critically weakened the Byzantine Empire especially, its territorial losses including the holy city of Jerusalem. But expansionism was also achieved through religious accommodation as much as it was by warfare. In most of the conquered territories, the Muslim rulers still permitted the practice of the Christian and Jewish faith by its adherents (there were also small numbers of Zoroastrians). They had to comply with restrictions to do so – a special *jizya*, or tax, was applied to non-Muslims and they were not allowed either to marry or attempt to convert a Muslim – but as long as they complied with such rules, they were allowed to live their lives under relative tolerance. This openness was even permitted, in fact especially so, in Jerusalem, which came under Muslim rule in 636 and largely remained so until the conquests of the First Crusade. The new Islamic rulers established their architectural stamp on the city, commissioning the Dome of the Rock in 691 (a shrine over the rock from which Muhammad is said to have ascended into heaven) and shortly after built the al-Aqsa Mosque a short distance away on Temple Mount, the mosque coming to be regarded as the third holiest site in Islam.

Nevertheless, Jerusalem and the Church of the Holy Sepulchre continued to hum with visiting Christian pilgrims from across the world, while Jews prayed against the Western Wall, also on

Below: The golden centrepiece of the Dome of the Rock in Jerusalem. According to Islamic tradition, Muhammad ascended to heaven from the site of the mosque.

Temple Mount. The three faiths largely worked around each other, side by side.

The greatest structural division within Islam, one that still exerts a critical influence on Middle Eastern politics to this day, occurred in the second half of the seventh century. Upon Muhammad's death in 632, authority over the Islamic world passed to the leaders (*caliphs*) of a caliphate, essentially a political-religious Muslim state/community. As the territorial boundaries of the Islamic world pushed further outwards, however, there were increasing internal tensions about the matter of leadership succession within the caliphate. The cracks widened, resulting in both conflict and a split into the Sunni and Shia branches of Islam. (Roughly explained, the Sunni regarded appointments of the caliphate as matter for majority decision by Muslim leaders, while the Shia believe their *imam*, or spiritual leader, is a hereditary successor of Muhammad, of which the first was Ali, Muhammad's cousin and son-in-law.)

Set against this backdrop of theological division, the tenth century was a time in which not only the *Dar al-Islam* split amongst itself, but also the relationship between Islam and the Christian world deteriorated. One of the major power players in Islam, the Abbasid dynasty ruling from the great city of Baghdad with three centuries of caliphs, began to lose its power from 909, when a rival dynasty, the Fatimids, broke away from their control and established a separate powerbase in Morocco, Algeria, Tunisia, Libya, Egypt and Palestine. The weakening of Abbasid control permitted the Byzantine reconquest of eastern Anatolia (including the subjugation of Armenia) and northern Syria (Antioch came back under Byzantine control in 969) and more and more parts of the Abbasid territory began to declare autonomy.

Below: Al-Hakim bi-Amr Allah was a Fatimid caliph (r. 996–1021). He was known for the ruthlessness and unpredictability of his behaviour.

The disturbed state of affairs in the Middle East made pilgrimage to the Holy Land a

Above: A painting showing the aftermath of the battle of Manzikert (1071), which saw the catastrophic defeat of a Byzantine army by Seljuk Muslims.

far more dangerous prospect, as pilgrims became subject to predation from warlords and opportunistic gangs. Later, in 1064–65, some 7,000–12,000 European pilgrims from Germany and Flanders, part of the 'Great German Pilgrimage', were attacked by prowling Bedouin bandits around Caesarea, during which some 5000 of their number were massacred. The relationship between Christians and Muslims in the Middle East also suffered moments of formal collapse. On 18 October 1009, the Fatimid ruler al-Hakim bi-Amr Allah capriciously overturned centuries of tolerance by ordering the destruction of the Church of the Holy Sepulchre in Jerusalem. Although subsequent Fatimid rulers did much to reverse the ill will generated by this event, it would remain as an historical dark shadow over Islamic and Christian relations.

But of all the forces that triggered the First Crusade, arguably the most significant was the rise of the Seljuk Turks, a warrior people from Central Asia and recent converts to Islam. The Seljuks were fervently expansionist, with their eye on both Byzantium's eastern territories and the lands of the weakened Abbasids. During the 1040s and 1050s the Abbasids were effectively conquered, or at least subjugated, by the Seljuk onslaught. The Seljuks also began making determined incursions into Anatolia, finding the area weakly garrisoned by Byzantine and Armenian forces. On 26 August 1071, Emperor Romanos IV Diogenes confronted a Seljuk army under the great sultan Alp Arslan at Manzikert with about 20,000 men, large numbers of his mercenary troops having already deserted, intimidated by the mobile style of cavalry warfare so nimbly practised by the Turks. The result was a catastrophic defeat for the imperial army, which suffered about 14,000 casualties.

Below: Statues of Sultan Alp Arslan and Malik Shah form part of the Independence Monument in Ashgabat, Turkmenistan. In Turkish, 'Alp Arslan' means 'Heroic Lion'.

Thereafter, the Byzantine control of Anatolia effectively collapsed as the Seljuks moved in, albeit in patchwork fashion, and with many major cities in the west of the region still under Byzantine remit. Nevertheless, such became the extent of the Seljuk reach over Anatolia that by 1077 they had even renamed it the Sultanate of Rum ('Rum' is the Seljuk spelling of the word 'Rome'). Antioch, Iconium (Konya) and Nicaea (Iznik) slipped from the Byzantine grasp, in terrible blows to the empire's prestige, contributing to internal conflicts that further weakened the Byzantine strength. Alp Arslan also then proceeded to conquer Mesopotamia, Syria and Palestine (including Jerusalem), up to the frontiers of Egypt; for the Fatimids, the Seljuks became a central threat to their power base.

For the Byzantines, the expansion of the Seljuk Turks was just one of the threats they faced during the second half of the eleventh century. (It is important to note that the wars with the Seljuks were far from the first conflicts between Byzantium and Muslim Arabs; Byzantine–Arab wars had actually been running intermittently since the late eighth century.) From the north, pagan tribes began making incursions across the River Danube in the 1050s, while Norman forces under Robert Guiscard took Byzantine territories in Italy in the early 1070s, and launched an invasion of the Byzantine Balkans in 1081.

BYZANTINE FIGHT-BACK

Facing threats on all sides, the Byzantine Empire might have appeared doomed to fall, but it was not to be. Many of the empire's enemies were fragmented rather than politically or militarily unified, not least the Seljuk Turks, divided between often rival warlords, some of whom even fought for the Byzantine cause. In fact, the recently crowned Byzantine emperor Alexios I (r. 1081–1115) bolstered a depleted army with vast numbers of mercenaries from across Europe, including Vikings, Anglo-Saxons, Venetians and Turks, plus the powerful naval assets of Venice. It was these resources that decisively crushed the pagans to the north, plus the fortuitous intervention of a typhoid epidemic that eventually stopped the Norman march on Constantinople (and killed Robert Guiscard), that saved the Byzantine Empire. In Anatolia, for a time Alexios even cooperated with Malik-Shah, the Seljuk sultan (son of Alp Arslan), to constrain the ambitions of adventurous Seljuk warlords in Anatolia, although Malik's power was largely nominal – the vizier Nizam al-Mulk was the de facto ruler – and both al-Mulk and Malik-Shah died within a month of each other in 1092, the former assassinated by dagger, the latter likely poisoned. Their deaths released the activities of the Seljuk warlords once more, who furthered their conquests in Anatolia.

ALEXIOS I BOLSTERED A DEPLETED ARMY WITH VAST NUMBERS OF MERCENARIES FROM ACROSS EUROPE, INCLUDING VIKINGS, ANGLO-SAXONS, VENETIANS AND TURKS.

With a larger mercenary army behind him, and no longer fighting a multi-front war, Alexios I could potentially have turned east and taken on the Seljuk Turks, with a reasonable chance of success. Yet he decided to look west for support in this enterprise, and in so doing opened the door to the First Crusade.

du lac et des fontaines qui sourdent
la environ. Et les murs estoient
fors haulx et espes & bien garnist.
et plains de grosses tours. Et se
en estoient les habitans fort legi-
ers & acoustumez de porter armes
et bien se monstrerent. Combi-
en que noz gens pour fortification quilz eussent ne laisserent
de fermer leur siege tout alentour

excepte de la partie du lac laquelle
ne peurent au premier assieger
dont leur venoit tousiours vivres
secours et nouvelles de Soli-
mand. Lequel se tenoit dedens
forestz a dix milles de Nicque
a tout son armee. espiant tousiours sil pourroit trouver son
point pour lever le siege de sa
Cite. et secourir ses gens. Aus-

1

THE FIRST CRUSADE

In 1095, ambassadors of Alexios I stood before a Church council in Piacenza, Italy, and presented their request for a European army to push back the Turkish tide. This army, however, would be like few others in Europe at this time, loyal principally to the papacy and motivated to a large degree by religious zeal and the desire to reclaim the Holy Land.

ALEXIOS' request carried with it a substantial package of potential risks, as well as rewards. Inviting a large foreign army, even as an ally, into Byzantine territory raised the prospect that ultimately self-interest and divisions would take over, and the foreigners would turn on the Byzantines. Historical sources have not left us with the nuances of Alexios' thoughts, nor his expectations of the exact extent or objectives of the crusaders. Certainly, he was fully intent on preserving the integrity of the Byzantine Empire, but by emphasizing the risk to Christendom, rather than to his empire, plus dangling the carrot of recovering the Holy Land, he bought Urban II onto his side.

So what was in it for the papacy? From our more secular age, we should not rule out genuine piety, at least as one ingredient.

Opposite: This medieval depiction of close-quarters combat during the bloody People's Crusade of 1096 graphically depicts something of the bloody nature of hand-to-hand fighting.

The threat to Western Christendom from Islam was perfectly proximate (Iberia) and the act of pilgrimage to the Holy Land, now made more perilous by roving Seljuk gangs, remained a pillar of demonstrated faith. Nor was the idea of a Crusade a new one. In 1074, for example, Pope Gregory VII had raised the idea of a military campaign into Anatolia to repel the Seljuks, although conflict with Henry IV prevented this becoming a practical reality. Two years later, Gregory promised indulgence for any Norman warriors who would fight to expel the Muslims from Sicily; in 1081 he even pledged heavenly rewards to the forces that helped him combat the German emperor.

Above: Alexios I Komnenos was the Byzantine Emperor from 1081–1118; his request for help fighting the Seljuk Turks helped galvanize the First Crusade.

Another important consideration for Urban II was that launching a Crusade would be a good way of distracting Western Europe away from constant internecine warfare with itself, and repurposing this militarism to distant lands. By focusing on an external threat, Europe might itself find greater peace and harmony.

DECLARING THE CRUSADE

Acceding to Alexios' request for support, now all Urban II had to do was raise an army of warriors, encouraging them, of their own volition, to leave their homes, march 5000km (3000 miles) across all manner of terrain, and fight a resilient and courageous foe. Supported by his capable representative, Adhémar, Bishop

POPE URBAN II'S SPEECH AT CLERMONT (AS RECORDED BY FULCHER OF CHARTRES)

ALTHOUGH, O sons of God, you have promised more firmly than ever to keep the peace among yourselves and to preserve the rights of the church, there remains still an important work for you to do. Freshly quickened by the divine correction, you must apply the strength of your righteousness to another matter which concerns you as well as God. For your brethren who live in the east are in urgent need of your help, and you must hasten to give them the aid which has often been promised them. For, as the most of you have heard, the Turks and Arabs have attacked them and have conquered the territory of Romania [the Greek empire] as far west as the shore of the Mediterranean and the Hellespont, which is called the Arm of St George. They have occupied more and more of the lands of those Christians, and have overcome them in seven battles. They have killed and captured many, and have destroyed the churches and devastated the empire. If you permit them to continue thus for awhile with impurity, the faithful of God will be much more widely attacked by them. On this account I, or rather the Lord, beseech you as Christ's heralds to publish this everywhere and to persuade all people of whatever rank, foot-soldiers and knights, poor and rich, to carry aid promptly to those Christians and to destroy that vile race from the lands of our friends. I say this to those who are present, it is meant also for those who are absent. Moreover, Christ commands it.

– Bongars, *Gesta Dei per Francos*, 1, pp. 382, Guibert of Nogent (1107–08)

Above: Francisco de Zurbaran – otherwise known as Pope Urban II – significantly strengthened the power of the papacy in Europe in 1088 to 1099.

et aultres sains lieux la enuiron.
Et les xpiens phabitans ⁊ demou
rans . ⁊ que les aultres par eulx
tyranniquement ⁊ inhumaine
ment tuez . Ilz auoient reserue
en infelicieuse vie afin que sur
eulx en lopprobre du saint nom
xpien peussent continuer plus
longuement leurs insaciables
cruaultez . Et comment ilz
les tenoient en trop opprobrieuse
captiuite ⁊ seruage . ou tresgrant
deshonneur ⁊ opprobre de tous
les xpiens . Concluant ⁊ mon
strant par diuerses raisons tres
euidentes que le saint peuple
xpien ne debuoit plus souffrir
ne endurer que les sains lieux et

of Le Puy, plus the warrior presence of Count Raymond of Toulouse (a man known as much for his godliness as for his competence with the sword), Urban set off to hold a special Church council at Clermont, Auvergne, in south-eastern France, where he would deliver a carefully crafted recruitment sermon. It took him two months to arrive in Clermont, and he preached the cause of the Crusade freely along the way, building up the word-of-mouth network and the energy behind his cause.

Opposite: Pope Urban II presides over the Council of Clermont, France, 1095, during which he declared that 'God wills it' for a Crusade to the East.

At the Second Council of Clermont, held between 18 and 28 November, and attended by more than 300 clerics and other European leaders, Urban delivered his case for a Crusade. Various versions of this speech have been transmitted down the ages, each with its own emphasis. That of Fulcher of Chartres, a priest who participated in the First Crusade and later wrote a chronicle of its events, is largely regarded as the most accurate, but all emphasized the following key points. First, the Christians of the Holy Land and the Byzantine Empire were under either threat or persecution from Islam, and subject to the most horrible violence. (There was a decent degree of exaggeration here.) Second, it was a Christian imperative for the West to go to Byzantium's aid as a fighting force, the campaign being a just war on account of its purpose of defending or freeing Christians from Muslim hordes. Third, and in an age when many people, high and low, often built up a long list of moral failings, this was appealing. Language was also critical. Note that the word 'Crusade' actually didn't begin to enter use until the thirteenth to fifteenth centuries. In 1095, Urban simply emphasized the well-understood concept of *peregrinato* (pilgrimage), albeit now a pilgrimage with the sword in hand.

Below: The Doge of Venice, Vitale Falier, invites citizens and soldiers to join the Crusade, c. 1095.

Below: Crusaders on the march. Horses were invaluable for the long-distance deployments, but their requirements for fodder further stretched logistics.

THE PEOPLE'S CRUSADE

Urban II's call to arms was a resounding success. Accurate figures are hard to come by, but in total it appears that as many as 100,000 people joined the First Crusade, mostly Franks from the French territories. (Later Crusades became far more international in flavour.) Both Alexios and Urban wanted hardened knights and soldiers above all else, men who could use their skill to beat the fast-moving Muslim cavalry and foot soldiers, and who could bring knowledge of siege warfare to bear on Muslim-held cities. Yet adventurism, piety, desire for wealth and land and, equally, potential escape from hardship, poverty and poor harvests, led thousands of regular civilians to join the Crusade, either individually or as family groups. As we shall see, the fact that crusading forces contained a high degree of non-combatants would cause no end of problems during the campaigns. An early indication of their vulnerability came with a forerunner of the 'official' crusade, known as the 'People's Crusade'.

The People's Crusade was a rather ad hoc adventure brought together by one Peter the Hermit, a charismatic priest and preacher from Amiens. Peter had previously attempted a pilgrimage to Jerusalem, although according to the account of Anna Comnena (a Byzantine princess, physician and historian) he had been prevented from reaching the city by the Seljuk Turks. There is some historical doubt whether he actually made this journey at all, but regardless, through impassioned preaching he managed to raise a crude army – a mixed host of soldiers and civilians – that numbered as many as 20,000, drawn from northern Europe and Germany. With the blessing of the Patriarch

Opposite: The Rhineland massacres of 1096 were a shameful early episode in the First Crusade. Here the army of German nobleman Volkmar and Count Emicho attack Merseburg, Germany.

of Jerusalem, Peter's army set off from Cologne for the Holy Land in late April/early May 1096; they would be joined by another similarly inspired force from southern France.

Early on in their journey, the People's Crusade demonstrated the brutal unpredictability of these religious armies. A large body of the crusaders, whipped into a frenzy by zealotry, decided to turn against a more proximate source of 'Christ's enemies' than the Muslims. In the Rhineland, the crusaders pounced upon the region's Jewish population, murdering thousands of them in outright bloodlust masquerading as piety. In Mainz alone, as many as 1100 were killed; those who survived mainly did so by paying off protectors, although as history showed even those who were paid could not always be trusted to back out of the deal when the crusaders turned up at the gates.

IN THE RHINELAND, THE CRUSADERS POUNCED UPON THE REGION'S JEWISH POPULATION, MURDERING THOUSANDS OF THEM IN OUTRIGHT BLOODLUST MASQUERADING AS PIETY.

The mob massacre of the Jews was an early indication of how vulnerable this religious group would be during the Crusades; further horrors would be visited upon them by the Christian armies during the subsequent centuries. The People's Crusade quickly revealed itself to be little more than an undisciplined rabble, one that Alexios watched with mounting concern as it approached his borders. In Hungary, the crusaders' raiding of local food supplies resulted in further heavy violence, with

Right: Peter the Hermit's 'People's Crusade' was wiped out by Turkish warriors in Anatolia. This artwork visually contrasts the supposed piety of the pilgrims with the predatory Muslims.

as many as 4000 Hungarians murdered, and the city of Belgrade, at that time part of the Kingdom of Hungary, burned down.

The worst excesses of the crusaders diminished somewhat within Byzantine borders, not least because Alexios made efforts to see that they were adequately fed. They reached positions near Constantinople, camping at Kibotos, where Alexios urged them to remain until the full strength of the crusading

Above: Peter the Hermit was known for being a highly capable orator and preacher, although he was ultimately not capable of controlling the army he raised.

forces could reach them from Europe. While Peter took note of the caution, other elements of the People's Crusade became impatient, and in September and October the army pushed on into Anatolia, and into the jaws of the Seljuks. While they were marching to Nicaea, they were ambushed on 21 October by a huge Turkish army, led by Kilij Arslan. Despite the courageous fighting by the military professionals among the crusaders, the battle turned into a horrifying and merciless rout, which spread into the largely civilian-manned camp behind the army's spearhead. All but 3000 individuals were killed.

The fate of the People's Crusade imparted the brutal and salutary lesson that faith alone would not protect the crusaders from the swords, arrows and spears of the Turks. Yet for all the professional elements within, Peter's army had been a crude and ultimately small one compared with what was to follow.

THE CRUSADING ARMIES

Those who committed themselves to the First Crusade, thereby becoming part of the *militia Christi*, did so making a solemn verbal oath that had, in those days, as much legal gravity as any written contract. Those who made the oath also received a cloth cross sewn onto their clothing, to mark them out as those embarking on the warrior pilgrimage, and giving rise to the expression 'to take the cross'.

The men, and many women, who formed the First Crusade came from a broad cross-section of society and status. They were organized, however, around a group of powerful European nobles, to be mentioned below. It is noteworthy, however, that the First

THE CRUSADER CROSS

At first, the cloth crosses sewn onto crusader clothing were of all manner of fabric, design and colour – the unexpected scale of volunteerism meant that there had been little chance of preparing anything approaching standard issue. As the Crusades progressed, however, the cross symbol became more formalized, and was even produced in different colours to denote specific nationalities – e.g. white for the British, red for the French, green for the Flemish. Throughout the campaigns, some particularly fervent crusaders might also draw or tattoo crosses on visible parts of their bodies, such as arms, chests or even foreheads. Other symbols of the crusaders were a humble wooden staff and a small purse; these were associated with the practice of pilgrimage, and thus they often appear in artwork from the time of the Crusades, even depictions of powerful rulers representing their humility by walking with these items.

Above: Godfrey of Bouillon (left), the Duke of Lower Lorraine (as Godfrey IV, 1089–1100) became the first Latin king of Jerusalem in 1099.

Crusade, despite its high profile and its deep connections with France, did not have the participation of the French king, Philip I, who had been excommunicated for his unorthodox marital relations. Nor did Henry IV take a leading role; this was, after all, a campaign led squarely by the Church, and supreme leadership from Europe's monarchy's was not needed. That said, the spectrum of leaders who headed the First Crusade did display a thorough mix of blue blood. The key figures were as follows:

Above: Robert II 'Curthose', Duke of Normandy from 1087 to 1106, was largely a failure in his administration of Normandy, but showed both courage and leadership during the First Crusade campaign.

Duke Robert II of Normandy – Also known by the epithet 'Curthose', meaning 'short stockings', Robert II of Normandy was the eldest son of William the Conqueror – it was William who is believed to have bestowed the 'Curthose' title. Robert became the Duke of Normandy upon his father's death in 1087, the same year in which his younger brother William became King William II of England. Robert attempted unsuccessfully to overthrow William from the throne, and by the time he later returned from the First Crusade his other brother Henry held the British crown, as Henry I.

Count Hugh of Vermandois – Being the brother of King Philip I of France, Count Hugh was the closest thing the First Crusade had to a French monarch. Indeed, Hugh was something of a surrogate king included to show French royal support for the Crusade, although it is said that he was convinced of his mission after witnessing an eclipse of the moon on 11 February 1096. He would not, however, distinguish himself during the Crusade.

Count Robert II of Flanders – Son of Robert I of Flanders, Robert II was a disciplined warrior and had a notable grasp of military strategy and tactics. He already had some connection to the Byzantine cause: his father had made a pilgrimage to Jerusalem in 1089, formed a friendship with Alexios and had even provided the Byzantines with a contingent of knights to fight against the Muslim forces.

Count Stephen of Blois – Stephen was the husband of Adela of Normandy, a powerful lady who also happened to be the daughter of William the Conqueror. Stephen was not a natural soldier, but any reticence about participating in the Crusades was overridden by the desire to please his wife, with inglorious consequences.

Above: Stephen of Blois was largely pressurized into joining the First Crusade. He would be killed fighting in the Holy Land in 1101.

Duke Godfrey of Bouillon – Duke Godfrey was a true soldier of Christ and he took a sizeable body of monks with him on the First Crusade to act as advisors. As the Duke of Lower Lorraine, Godfrey had previously demonstrated loyalty to Henry IV during the Investiture Controversy, in which he showed his military prowess, but later signed up to the papal cause, becoming one of the most potent of the Crusade's leaders.

Baldwin of Boulogne – The brother of Godfrey of Bouillon, Baldwin was an ambitious and contradictory personality, given to bouts of both penance and sin in equal measure. Godfrey and Baldwin were also accompanied by their other brother, Eustace.

Count Raymond IV of Toulouse – Raymond was the senior figure among the crusading leadership, being in his late 50s at the time of the First Crusade and exhibiting polished skills in both warfare and diplomacy, which gave him a high status in the eyes of Urban II. Raymond was also a deeply religious man, with an expressed wish to die in the Holy Land, hence his enthusiastic embrace of the crusading cause.

Prince Bohemund of Taranto – Bohemund was a ruthless Norman, the son of Robert Guiscard. A warrior through and through, not only had Bohemund's father fought against the Byzantines in Italy, Bohemund had also participated in the campaigns, including those in the Balkans. The primary motivation for his shift in priorities was likely wealth; he had not received a substantial inheritance following his father's death, and so was looking to make his fortune elsewhere. His presence on the Crusade can scarcely have been reassuring to Alexios, who, along with his daughter Anna Comnena, despised the rough Norman.

Above: Bishop Adhémar of Le Puy, papal legate of the First Crusade. Adhémar had previously made a non-military pilgrimage to the Holy Land, in 1086–87.

Bishop Adhémar of Le Puy – Already introduced above, Bishop Adhémar was essentially Pope Urban II's loyal representative on the First Crusade, a man who could act as an intermediary and consultant between the Pope and the complex spectrum of leaders who were heading the crusading army.

These men, and others like them (in total there were about 200 individual lords), headed a crusading force that numbered up to 100,000. Some 6000 knights provided the mounted cavalry, the mobile shock force of the army, while there were around 45,000 foot soldiers, split between the wealthier individuals who provided their own weaponry, down to the lowest foot-sloggers who were given basic tools of war. The rest of the mass consisted of civilians of all descriptions, not only the families of some of the warriors (many hoped that they would build a new family life in the east), but also a large body of servants, merchants and assorted pilgrims, many of whom brought little to the campaign except their faith and aspiration. It was also an intensely cosmopolitan army, containing more than 20 different language groups. It was clear from the outset that strategic coordination between all the different elements was to be an issue.

ALEXIOS EARNESTLY WANTED TO PREVENT THE CRUSADERS LOOTING TOWNS AND VILLAGES ON THE WAY, ACTIONS THAT COULD LEAD TO RESISTANCE AND LOCALIZED CONFLICT.

The First Crusade would rely heavily upon the support of Alexios I. The Crusades were financially onerous endeavours, and European coffers were often already stretched to breaking point by intermittent wars elsewhere. Alexios had pledged to feed the crusaders within his territory. This was a matter of pragmatism and not necessarily good will;

Alexios earnestly wanted to prevent the crusaders looting towns and villages on the way, actions that could lead to resistance and localized conflict. In fact, all crusaders would be the beneficiaries of the emperor's wider largesse, receiving gifts of money and goods according to their station; the nobles who arrived in Constantinople would be veritably showered with wealth.

The trade-off for this support, without which the Crusade stood no chance of success, was a pledge of loyalty to Alexios, the crusaders making the commitment that Byzantine territories captured from the Muslims would immediately be handed over to the emperor's representatives. This pledge did not clear up all possible ambiguities, however, as many cities and territories – e.g. those in Palestine and Syria – had been so long in Muslim hands that it was unclear whether they still fell under the Byzantine purview. As we shall see, there was still much room for manoeuvre.

In addition to his financial and logistical benefactions, Alexios would also provide some military support, although the loss of manpower from the Anatolian heartlands meant that his human resources were reduced. Some 2000 Byzantine troops under the commander Tatikios would accompany the crusaders, at least for part of their campaign.

Below: The scene as the forces of Robert Curthose depart on the First Crusade. Robert would not see France again for another four years.

As well as providing a combat contribution, Tatikios was also partly there to guarantee that the crusaders kept their word about handing over captured territories back to the Byzantines.

Opposite: Fatimid warriors ride out from a fortified town to attack crusader siege forces, as depicted in a twelfth-century Egyptian mural.

MUSLIM FORCES

Facing the crusaders was a collection of Muslim forces, distributed between Anatolia and North Africa. As noted above, the armies of Islam were at this time by no means a united front, but rather a number of regional groupings and warlords, broadly united according to their territorial and religious allegiance. Among the Seljuk Turks, the armies had a somewhat informal nature, and were typically small, about 10,000–15,000 men. Rather than having standing armies, the Seljuk forces typically consisted of a small *askar* – essentially a professional bodyguard force recruited from *ghulans* or *mamluks*, slaves or prisoners of war – supported by *ajnad* provincial troops and *ahdath* urban militias. *Askar* cavalry, known for their skill with bow and sword from horseback, formed another elite within the Muslim armies. When necessary, which it often was, the Seljuk armies were padded out heavily with mercenaries.

Above: This thirteenth-century relief shows Turkish warriors. They wear the *hazagand*, a heavy cotton tunic sometimes with mail attached.

Because of the Seljuks' rolling military activity, they had some very experienced commanders in charge. Kilij Arslan I, for example, was the Seljuk ruler of Anatolia at the time of the First Crusade and was one of the key figures in the defeat of the ill-advised People's Crusade. Despite his crushing of this effort, Kilij Arslan was generally regarded as a judicious and surprisingly tolerant ruler, as much interested in resolving tensions through diplomacy as through violence. Lesser governors included Yaghi Siyan of the territory around Antioch, Ridwan Ibn Tutush of Aleppo and Kür-Bugha of Aleppo. Of these three, Ridwan has been particularly singled out in Islamic history as one who opportunistically sought alliances and advantages to the detriment of the overall Muslim war effort. Certainly, Ridwan was comfortable crossing the Sunni/Shia divide, at times making accommodations with Syrian and Fatimid Shia regimes.

The Fatimids have an interesting relation to this First Crusade, as in many ways, at least at the beginning of the conflict, the Fatimid caliphate was more of an ally than an enemy, united with the Byzantines against the Seljuk Turks. Indeed, Alexios actually informed the Fatimids that the crusaders were coming, and even well into the First Crusade, right up to the point that the crusaders took Ascalon, the Fatimid leaders attempted to make settlements with the invaders.

The Fatimids had a relatively small professional Arab army, but one that could be padded out to great size with large numbers of mercenary Berbers, Bedouin, Africans (especially Sudanese), Armenians and Daylamites (a people from the mountainous regions of northern Iran). There were even some reports of Frankish soldiers being in the service of the Fatimids. The de facto supreme leader of the Fatimid caliphate at the time of the First Crusade was the Grand Vizier al-Afdal Ibn Badr al-Jamali, a sophisticated, intelligent and diplomatic ruler, who governed from 1089 through to his assassination in 1121.

THE FIGHT FOR ANATOLIA

In August 1096, after months of preparations, the armies of the First Crusade began their epic movements down through Europe. The overall army split into four main contingents, headed respectively by Godfrey of Bouillon, Raymond of Toulouse, Robert of Normandy, Stephen of Blois (amongst others) and Bohemund of Taranto. Setting out from different destinations and at different times, the crusading armies moved down through the Balkans and eventually converged on Constantinople between December 1096 and April 1097.

At the beginning of May, the crusaders finally began to take the fight to their enemies, as they crossed the Bosphorus into Anatolia. Their first objective was Nicaea, a city with spiritual resonance for the crusaders, as it was here that the Nicene Creed – the first Christian statement of faith – had been drawn up by the General Council of the Church in 325. The vanguard of the crusading force, headed by Godfrey of Bouillon and Robert of Flanders, had reached and invested the city by 6 May, with heavy reinforcements from Count Raymond arriving about a week later on 14 May. Two days later, Kilij Arslan arrived in force, having gathered an army and marched with due haste across Anatolia, confident that he could deal with the new threat in the same way that he had dealt with the People's Crusade. Kilij Arslan hurled his mostly mounted troops against a crusading encampment just outside the southern wall of the city. Yet although the Turkish cavalry assaulted with commitment, shocking their adversaries with both their mobility and the accuracy of their archery, the crusaders stood firm, aided by numerical superiority and a strip of terrain that limited the Seljuks' overall manoeuvrability. At the critical moment, Godfrey of Bouillon and Robert of Flanders led the

KILIJ ARSLAN HURLED HIS MOSTLY MOUNTED TROOPS AGAINST A CRUSADING ENCAMPMENT JUST OUTSIDE THE SOUTHERN WALL OF THE CITY.

Left: At the siege of Nicaea (May–June 1097), crusaders appear to launch human heads at the battlements using trebuchets.

autres batailles iusques a
.iiij. Et depuis ẽsuient toutes
fois la derraine qui estoit buy
mont.
La veissiez fier chapleis
des espees. Li marteleis estoit
estoit si grãs q̃ on ne pooit oir

desconfite. Li autre s'en est
maleoient mout. Il guen
cele part : o toute sa batail
le. Et si feri mout vigue
reusement. Illoec en decau
perent tant. q̃ toute la ter
en fu ionchie des mors. Il

q̃ les se contenoient foiblemẽt.
Il aprocha ⁊ vit la bataille
buymont qui n'estoit mie
encore assamblee. Il assã
bla a lui. mlt por tant ⁊ lan
ce. Puis coururent as espees
⁊ as coutiaux. Li turc furẽt

troops forward in a flanking attack that finally routed Kilij Arslan's army and put it to flight.

While Kilij Arslan, now more respectful of his enemy, regrouped and began to gather a larger army, the crusaders continued their onslaught against Nicaea, using a clattering spectrum of siege engines to batter the fortifications constantly with stones and arrows. Finally, on 19 June, Nicaea surrendered, its inhabitants and defenders having suffered terrible casualties from both combat and deprivation. Much to the chagrin of the victorious crusaders, Alexios had banned looting from the city, although the emperor compensated the European soldiers well from his own coffers.

A week after the fall of Nicaea, the crusading army resumed its march south, albeit now into massive and separate columns, a group of 20,000 troops under Robert of Normandy, Stephen of Blois, Bohemund and Tancred (an Italo-Norman leader), followed by 30,000 men commanded by Godfrey of Bouillon, Raymond of Toulouse, Robert of Flanders and Hugh of Vermandois. The march took them through long expanses of arid, exposed wilderness; exhaustion, heat and disease now began their cruel, patient work on the crusading host, on both humans and animals alike. The crusaders were also now far more exposed to a sudden attack by a refreshed Kilij Arslan, and the onslaught came against the column of 20,000 troops on 1 July 1097 in or around (there is some historical debate over the exact location) the long valley of Dorylaeum.

THE MARCH TOOK THEM THROUGH LONG EXPANSES OF ARID, EXPOSED WILDERNESS; EXHAUSTION, HEAT AND DISEASE NOW BEGAN THEIR CRUEL, PATIENT WORK ON THE CRUSADING HOST...

The Christian leaders had received some advance warning of the impending attack, and were encamped by the side of marshy ground to provide flanking protection against the Turkish cavalry. Nevertheless, the Seljuk onslaught came with nearly overwhelming power, the ferocious mounted attacks driving back the crusaders' own cavalry, resulting in a desperate close-range defence of the camp. Everyone was involved in the battle, with women and children performing vital logistical roles, bringing

Opposite: This French manuscript illumination depicts the defeat of the Turks at the battle of Dorylaeum on 1 July 1097. The victory for the crusaders provided a huge moral boost for the Christian forces.

up supplies and water for the fighters. Despite being on the back foot, the crusaders had some advantages. Bohemund in particular had constructed a tight defence, one that the Turkish troops failed to break, plus the heavy plate and mail armour worn by the soldiers – so cumbersome and heavy on the march – now proved superbly resistant to the impacts of enemy arrows and swords. After holding out for five hours, the defenders were finally joined by the larger crusading force of 30,000 men, and the day was saved. Kilij Arslan was once again compelled to retreat, although as a commander he had limited control over an army representing various regional interests.

The crusader victories at both Nicaea and Dorylaeum had an energizing effect on morale, and the army pressed on into the Anatolian interior towards its next major objective, the great city of Antioch, some 500km (310 miles) away. It was now that divisions of self-interest in both sides began to reveal themselves in earnest. Kilij Arslan, his reputation tainted by two major defeats, struggled to present a unified Muslim front, and the crusaders met a reduced resistance as they pushed forward. Thus one of the major centres of Seljuk power in Anatolia, the city of Iconium (modern Konya), was abandoned by the Turks and occupied without a fight. On the crusaders' side, meanwhile, an ambitious Baldwin of Boulogne detached himself from the main army and headed east towards Edessa, a city headed by the Armenian prince Thoros. He had

Above: Baldwin, later the first King of Jerusalem, enters the city of Edessa in 1098; he had already forced the abdication of the city's ruler, Thoros.

requested crusading assistance against the Turks, which was provided by Baldwin. With uncanny timing, Thoros was then killed shortly afterwards during an uprising, and Baldwin became the new Count of Edessa in March 1098.

INTO SYRIA – THE SIEGE OF ANTIOCH

Having advanced across Anatolia, the crusaders then turned south into Syria. They had every right to be confident of the future, but having already advanced many hundreds of miles, mostly on foot, they were not the army that had set out from Constantinople several months previously. For a start, the numbers had dropped significantly, to about 25,000 all told. This depletion was not just on account of the attrition of disease and battle, but also from the reality of campaign life resulting in many reconsidering their military pilgrimage and turning back for home. Nevertheless, Antioch was reached on 21 October 1097.

25,000 CRUSADERS WERE STILL INSUFFICIENT TO ESTABLISH A TOTALLY SECURE PERIMETER, MEANING THAT SUPPLIES WERE STILL ABLE TO ENTER THE CITY THROUGHOUT THE SIEGE.

Antioch, defended by the warriors of Yaghi Siyan, was a formidable objective even for a European army familiar with the practices of siege warfare. The walls of the city were of such extent – a total of 10km (6 miles) in length – that the 25,000 crusaders were still insufficient to establish a totally secure perimeter, meaning that supplies were still able to enter the city throughout the siege. Conversely, the situation still looked difficult for the Muslim defenders. Through establishing numerous strongpoints in Anatolia, the crusaders essentially controlled the northern approaches; the only relief from the south could potentially be provided by the Fatimids, but at this stage of the Crusade they still had no interest in assisting the Turks. Furthermore, the crusader commanders enjoyed naval dominance over the Mediterranean, with Genoese shipping in particular bringing in both fresh men and supplies through various ports captured on the eastern Mediterranean coastline. The crusaders also set about the siege with some mechanical ingenuity. They built a large barbican tower at a key point

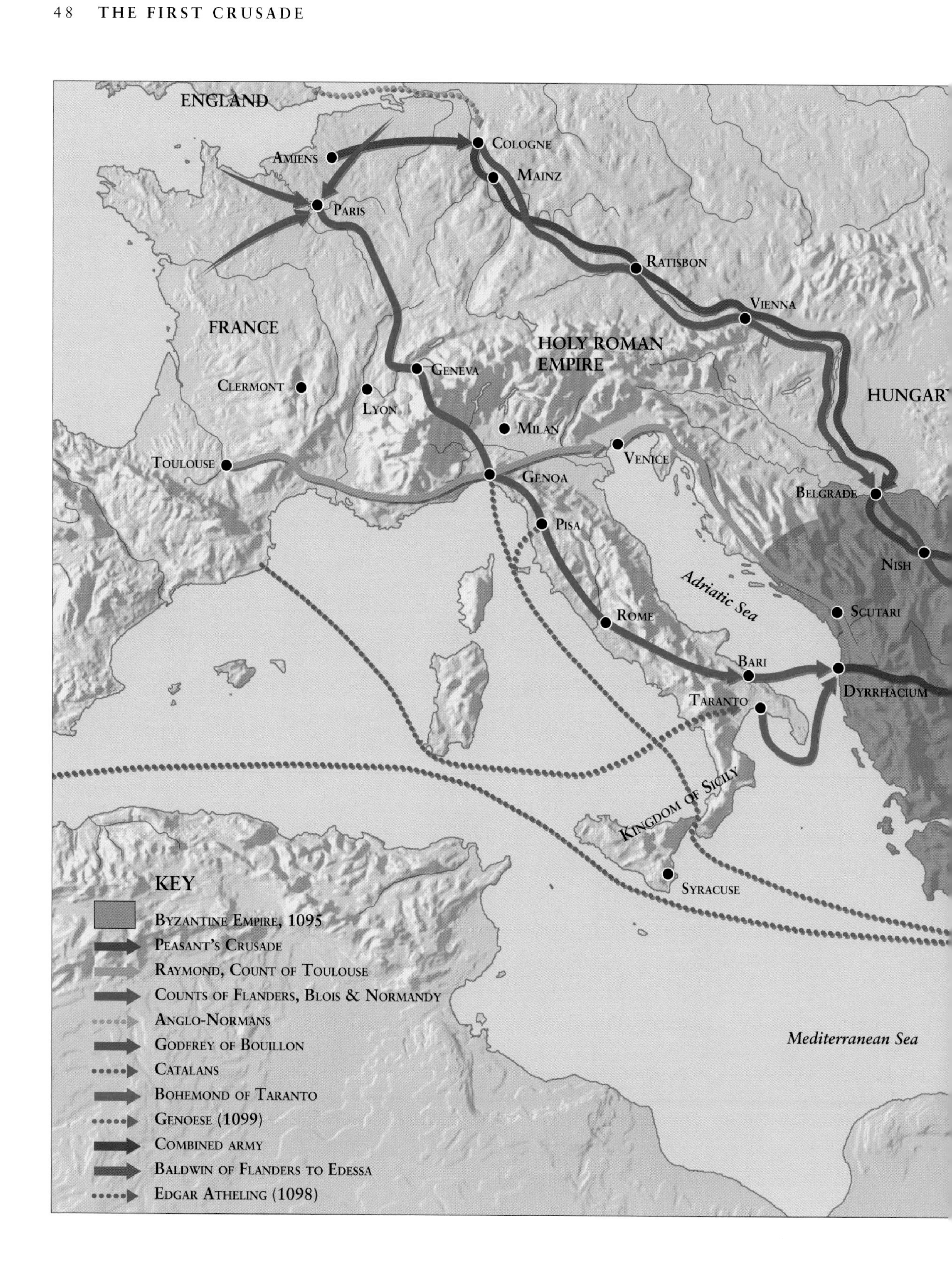
ENGLAND
Amiens
Cologne
Mainz
Paris
Ratisbon
Vienna
FRANCE
HOLY ROMAN EMPIRE
Geneva
Clermont
Lyon
HUNGARY
Milan
Toulouse
Venice
Genoa
Belgrade
Pisa
Nish
Adriatic Sea
Scutari
Rome
Bari
Dyrrhacium
Taranto
Kingdom of Sicily
Syracuse
Mediterranean Sea
KEY
Byzantine Empire, 1095
Peasant's Crusade
Raymond, Count of Toulouse
Counts of Flanders, Blois & Normandy
Anglo-Normans
Godfrey of Bouillon
Catalans
Bohemond of Taranto
Genoese (1099)
Combined army
Baldwin of Flanders to Edessa
Edgar Atheling (1098)

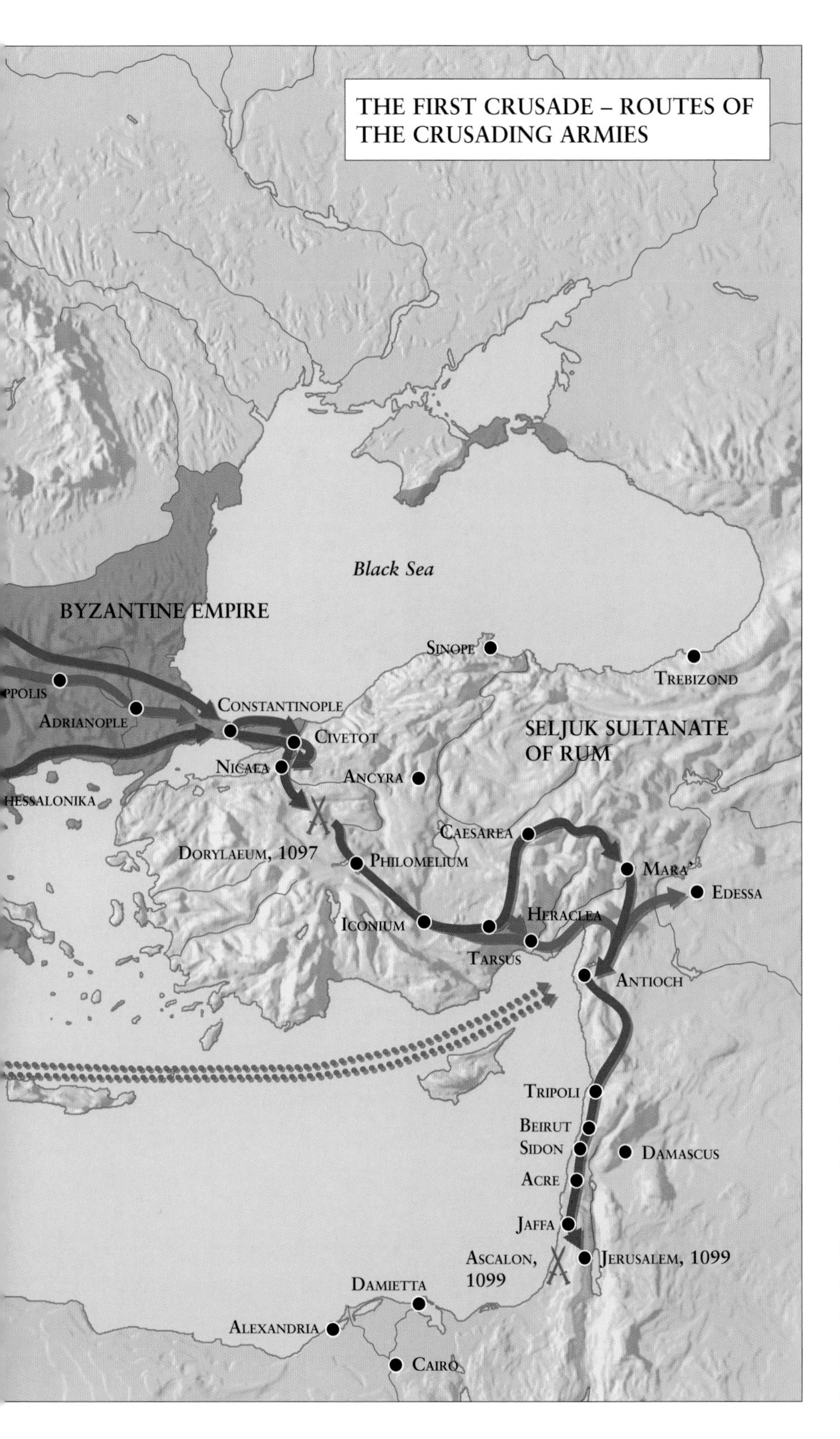

Left: This map shows the route taken by the various Crusader forces to reach the Holy Land. Although France provided the bulk of the troops for the First Crusade, the Crusaders were a truly multinational force, with elements from England, Catalonia, Italy and the Rhineland.

outside the walls, as a means of preventing localized Turkish raids, plus they also constructed a major pontoon bridge from the east bank of the River Orontes (the river that formed the western and the northern borders of the city) and the critical port of St Symeon on the west bank.

Below: The supposed finding of the 'Holy Lance', the spear that was used to pierce Christ's body on the cross. The Lance was carried by Adémar in battle.

To a large extent, the outcome of a siege is dictated by time and not by combat. For the crusaders now found themselves enduring months of miserable winter weather, shivering under rains and biting winds. Disease carried away the lives of the Europeans with daily frequency. Stomachs were also frequently empty, as the influx of supplies through the ports (compounded by the medieval problems of storing and transporting fresh food) proved inadequate to the scale of victualling required. The crusaders constantly sent out foraging trips into the interior, but the barren nature of the surrounding landscape plus the dangers of predatory attacks by Turkish forces, meant that they frequently returned empty-handed.

Desertion and fragmentation began to take hold by the early months of 1098, as morale plunged. Bishop Adhémar urged the crusaders on to greater personal piety, to a large degree blaming sinfulness for their plight. Robert

of Normandy and Tatikios left the siege altogether, the former heading out to the fort of Laodicea (Latakya) and the latter going back to Constantinople, to persuade Alexios to send further assistance.

Above: The crusader leader Bohemund of Taranto was a archetypal Christian warrior, physically and emotionally strong. One contemporary of Bohemund described him as a 'wonderful spectacle'.

Despite their troubles, the crusaders around Antioch still demonstrated a capacity for intelligent initiative. For example, having got wind of a major Muslim relief army, commanded by Ridwan of Aleppo, camped at nearby Harenc, Bohemund rode out with a relatively small cavalry force and inflicted a defeat upon the surprised Muslims, one that bought the crusaders the time and space to tighten their grip upon Antioch itself. But it was imperative that they bring the siege to a quick conclusion. New intelligence revealed that an even larger Muslim relief army, commanded by the ruler of Mosul, Kerbogha, was on its way. Given the crusaders' weak state, this news clearly indicated a pressing existential threat. Stephen of Blois, a man whose heart never entirely belonged to the Crusade in the first place, deserted the siege and took his troops with him on 2 June. With supreme irony, on his way back north and east Stephen even met Alexios at the head of reinforcements, but convinced the emperor that the siege was a lost cause, and so the Byzantine troops turned back. But by the time this occurred, matters around Antioch had moved on.

Although the crusaders conducted the military aspect of the siege competently, in the end it was treachery that allowed them to break into the city itself. Some defecting Muslim troops on the outer defences aided a small group of crusaders in climbing over the walls; the crusaders then opened a main gate, and in flooded the warriors from outside. Under the red glow of night-time torches, a hellish scene unfolded as the vengeful crusaders massacred thousands of Muslims, and even hundreds of Antioch's Christians in the confusion.

One crusader, Peter Bartholomew, claimed that he received a vision from God, urging all Christian warriors to acts of repentance.

Antioch had now fallen, but the crusaders inside now became the besieged, as Kerbogha's army advanced in from the east and laid its own siege from late in the afternoon of 4 June. Mindful that they could expect no mercy if they fell to Kerbogha, many crusaders (particularly civilians) chose the path of desertion, slipping out of the city at night and trying to make their way to safety further north. Just when all might have appeared lost, there occurred one of those curious events so typical of the age. One crusader, Peter Bartholomew, claimed that he received a vision from God, urging all Christian warriors to acts of repentance; if they did so, God would enable Peter to find an object proving His blessing. Subsequently, on 15 June, Peter, spiritually guided to a spot just outside St Peter's church in Antioch, dug up and discovered the fragment of a spear, which was regarded as the 'Holy Lance' that had pierced Christ's side as he hung on the cross. Galvanized by this blessing, on 28 June the crusaders – weak from months of a starvation diet and heavily outnumbered by the enemy – opened the gates of Antioch and ventured out in a surprise attack, most of the men moving on foot (almost all the horses and oxen had died by this point). Led by the redoubtable Bohemund, and with Adhémar confidently brandishing the Holy Lance, the crusaders

MUSLIM BOWS

IN CONTRAST TO THE long, relatively straight self-bows (made from a single piece of wood) typically used by archers in Western Europe at this time, the Turkish and Arab troops relied upon short composite bows, often with a highly accentuated recurve. Unlike self-bows, composite bows utilize a mixture of materials in their construction. A common bow example would have a core of high-quality wood, such as poplar, maple or ash, but with a laminate of animal horn glued to the belly of the bow (the side facing the archer) and animal sinew on the front. When the bow was drawn, the animal horn was compressed while the sinew was stretched, these two effects maximizing the energy that was then stored up in the bow to power the release. Adding a recurve further increased the power. A well-made composite bow, despite being relatively short (usually around 1–1.4m/3–4 ½ft in length), still had an effective range of some 200m (656ft), although when fired at optimal elevation they could reach out well beyond that distance, albeit at the cost of accuracy. The main disadvantages of composite bows lay in their production method – they took much time and proper materials to build, both of which could be lacking on a campaign. They were also more prone to malfunctions than self-bows, especially in damp weather, which could weaken the animal glue holding together the laminations.

Below: Saracens assault Constantinople in this Byzantine manuscript, with Muslim archers laying down accurate suppressing fire against the defenders on the battlements.

rushed out, each column of troops stretching out into the line as soon as they had crossed over onto the opposite side of the Orontes River, maximizing their front. Through a remarkable combination of tactical handling by Bohemund, outright courage, and destabilizing tribal divisions within Kerbogha's army, the crusaders managed to pull off a remarkable victory, even overrunning Kerbogha's camp as the Muslim forces fled in retreat. If ever a sign was needed that God was on the side of the Crusade, this appeared to be it.

Below: The legendary Saint George was meant to have appeared supernaturally during several crusader battles. Here he manifests on the Mount of Olives near Jerusalem, in 1099.

THE MARCH TO JERUSALEM

Following the double victory at Antioch, it could be expected that the crusaders would immediately have resumed their march south, to expedite the capture of Jerusalem. In fact, there now followed an unedifying period of political manoeuvring and in-fighting. Regarding Jerusalem, it was the Fatimids who actually made one of the boldest moves, when the Grand Vizier al-Afdal – sensing that the time had now come to take some protective actions against the crusader advance – led an army north into

Palestine and seized the city from the Seljuks. The Turks were now a fractured people, and not capable of making unified strategic decisions.

For the Crusade, it appeared for a time that its leaders could not collect themselves in common purpose. There were arguments about whether Antioch should be given back to the Byzantine Empire – Bohemund wanted to retain the city as ruler, whereas Raymond of Toulouse advocated an imperial handover, likely because he was close to Alexios and could expect a substantial reward. Bishop Adhémar died from disease on 1 August 1098, and both Alexios and Pope Urban II refused pleas from some knights that they come to Antioch and take personal charge of the Crusade. In the power play, further campaigning moved the chess pieces around on the board. For example, on 11 May 1098 Raymond captured the city of Ma'rat al-Nu'man, about 80km (50 miles) south-east of Antioch, consolidating his hold over the territory. This action culminated in another ghastly massacre of the city's population.

Below: Raymond IV of Toulouse was one of the more genuinely pious Crusader leaders, plus a competent military commander.

The general mass of the crusaders steadily grew more tired with the behaviour of the leaders. They had not come this far, and suffered so greatly, to let Jerusalem now slip from their grasp. Raymond came to be identified as the one to lead the Crusade southward, and so in mid-January 1099 – barefoot to show his penitence – Raymond departed with an army of crusaders towards Jerusalem, soon joined by the men of Tancred, Robert of Normandy, Robert of Flanders and Godfrey of Lorraine. The total manpower of the force was in the region of 12,000–14,000 men, about 1300 of that number being knights, the rest foot soldiers. Bohemund stayed behind in his prize, Antioch.

As the crusaders marched, the population and garrison of Jerusalem began preparations for its defence, under the guidance of the city's governor, Iftikhar al-Dawla. To ensure the integrity of the defence, Christian inhabitants of the city were expelled (Jews were allowed to stay). Essential materials were stockpiled – timber (for constructing engines), water, food, animals, weaponry – while outside the walls water sources were polluted to prevent their use by the besiegers.

THE SIEGE OF JERUSALEM

The crusading army marching down to Jerusalem experienced little in the way of resistance. On their way they passed through many places that would become landmarks in the crusader states: Tripoli, Beirut, Tyre, Jaffa, Ramla and Bethlehem – the latter was captured by Tancred and Gaston on 6 June, a day before the crusaders

Below: Crusaders suffer the agonies of thirst during their campaign. Water logistics were a constant problem for the Christian campaigns in the Holy Land.

reached Jerusalem itself and began their siege. The crusaders also conducted a minor siege of the city of Arqa, although they abandoned this without result on 13 May.

The first sight of Jerusalem was a wrenching moment for many of the crusaders. Numbers of them wept openly, sensing that their ordeal of faith was now about to reach its ultimate conclusion. And yet, much suffering still lay before them. A contemporary eyewitness of the siege explained a little of the reality of life outside the city walls:

'WE SEWED UP SKINS OF OXEN AND BUFFALOES IN WHICH WE BROUGHT THE WATER SIX MILES. THE WATER WE DRANK FROM SUCH RECEPTACLES WAS FETID.'

> *During the siege we were unable to find any bread to buy for about the space of ten days, until a messenger came from our ships; also we were afflicted by great thirst, so much so that in fear and terror we had to water our horses and other animals six miles away. The fountain of Siloam, at the foot of Mount Sion, sustained us, but the water was sold among us at a high price... We sewed up skins of oxen and buffaloes in which we brought the water six miles. The water we drank from such receptacles was fetid, and what with foul water and barley bread we daily suffered great affliction and distress. Moreover, the Saracens hid near all the springs and wells and ambushed our men, killing and mutilating them and driving off the animals into their dens and caverns.*

In terms of their dispositions around the city, Robert of Flanders, Godfrey of Bouillon and Robert of Normandy positioned their men around the northern half of the perimeter; Raymond of Toulouse took the south. One of the key early problems faced was the lack of local timber to build siege engines; much of the surrounding landscape had been stripped of timber by the city garrison, who had subsequently constructed engines in greater number and quality than those possessed by the attackers.

It would take a full week of action for the crusaders to gain the upper hand. The aforementioned eyewitness to the siege here continues the story:

Opposite: In this depiction of the siege of Jerusalem, crusader troops prepare to fire a siege engine, a mix of catapult and trebuchet that seems historically inaccurate.

Then our leaders planned to attack the city with machines, in order to enter it and adore the sepulchre of our Saviour. They made two wooden towers and many other machines... Day and night on the fourth and fifth days of the week we vigorously attacked the city on all sides; but before we made our assault the bishops and priests persuaded all by their preaching and exhortation that a procession should be made round Jerusalem to God's honour, faithfully accompanied by prayers, alms and fasting. Early on the sixth day we attacked the city on all sides and could do nothing against it. We were all surprised and alarmed. Then, at the approach of the hour at which our Lord Jesus Christ deigned to undergo the passion of the cross for us, our knights in one of the towers fought bravely, amongst them Duke Godfrey and his brother, Count Eustace.

One of our knights, Letholdus by name, climbed on to the wall of the city. When he reached the top, all the defenders of the city quickly fled along the walls and through the city. Our men followed and pursued them, killing and hacking, as far as the temple of Solomon, and there was such a slaughter that our men were up to their ankles in the enemy's blood...

THE IMMEDIATE AFTERMATH WAS A NOW LEGENDARY BLOODLETTING, AS POSSIBLY TENS OF THOUSANDS OF PEOPLE WERE KILLED IN THE STREETS AND IN THEIR HOMES IN THE MOST BESTIAL MANNER.

Some details are missing from this account. For example, an important element in the successful outcome of the siege was a Genoese and English maritime force that anchored in the port of Jaffa, providing not only crucial supplies but also the technical expertise of the sailors, who assisted in constructing the siege engines.

Jerusalem finally succumbed to the crusaders on 15 July 1099. The immediate aftermath was a now legendary bloodletting, as possibly tens of thousands of people were killed in the streets and in their homes in the most bestial manner. The murdered were not only the unfortunate Muslims, but also large numbers of Jews.

THE SACK OF JERUSALEM – Fulcher of Chartres

When the pagans saw one standard planted on the wall, they were completely demoralized, and all their former boldness vanished, and they turned to flee through the narrow streets of the city. Those who were already in rapid flight began to flee more rapidly. Count Raymond and his men, who were attacking the wall on the other side, did not yet know of all this, until they saw the Saracens leap from the wall in front of them. Forthwith, they joyfully rushed into the city to pursue and kill the nefarious enemies, as their comrades were already doing. Some Saracens, Arabs, and Ethiopians took refuge in the tower of David, others fled to the temples of the Lord and of Solomon. A great fight took place in the court and porch of the temples, where they were unable to escape from our gladiators. Many fled to the roof of the temple of Solomon, and were shot with arrows, so that they fell to the ground dead. In this temple almost ten thousand were killed. Indeed, if you had been there you would have seen our feet coloured to our ankles with the blood of the slain. But what more shall I relate? None of them were left alive; neither women nor children were spared.

– From Bongars, *Gesta Dei per Francos*, Guibert of Nogent (1107–08)

Left: The looting of Jerusalem after its capture by the crusaders. The possibility of acquiring new wealth would have been an implicit motivation for many of the participants in the First Crusade.

Left: Another scene from the capture of Jerusalem in 1099. Note how the attackers are using siege ladders and siege towers (equipped with fold-down walkways) to ascend or cross the city walls.

Details of such behaviour would eventually filter through to Western Europe, although it would take weeks and months to do so. Many senior clergy expressed their horror at what had occurred on the streets of the holiest city in Christendom. More significantly, however, was the fact that the butchery of Muslims in Jerusalem led to a hardening, and to a limited extent unification, of the Islamic world. Nothing unifies a diverse people more than a merciless common threat.

Ignoring the bloody afternote, however, the Christian world rejoiced that Jerusalem was now back in its control, for the first time since the seventh century. With impressive timing, Pope Urban II actually died two weeks following the recapture of the city, and such was the slow transfer of information in those days that he never actually knew about the final victory of the Crusade that he had put in place.

2

Crusader States: Life, People and Politics

The Crusader States established following the victorious First Crusade opened up a new world for settlers from Europe. They were places of opportunity, with potential for wealth, trade and a high standard of living, and one in which all faiths, for a time, lived side-by-side in an imperfect understanding.

The conquest of Jerusalem did not bring peace through victory. Indeed, within weeks of the siege's conclusion, the crusader forces turned to face a new threat. During the siege, the Fatimid Grand vizier al-Afdal assembled a large relief force, which marched north in June but was still short of Jerusalem by the time the city fell. Thus, in early August it was encamped just outside the city of Ascalon, about 80km (50 miles) south of Jerusalem. Al-Afdal, perhaps

Opposite: The appointment of Godfrey of Bouillon as the King of Jerusalem in July 1099. Some crusader leaders made entirely new lives in the Levant, never returning to Europe again.

hoping that centuries of Muslim and Christian accommodation could be preserved, now seemed to do little more than send a letter of protest regarding the post-siege massacre. The crusaders, however, riding on the energy of a string of victories, assembled a 10,000-strong army under Godfrey of Bouillon's overall command and marched out to attack the Fatimids. Using an innovative tactical formation, albeit one likely influenced by Turkish or Central Asian precedents, Godfrey imposed a major defeat on the Fatimids, their troops put into flight, many of them hunted down and slaughtered in the wooded groves on the eastern side of Ascalon. Al-Afdal, and the traumatized remnants of his army, now retreated back to the city, where they were evacuated from the port by naval vessels. The city authorities, recognizing that they were now at the crusaders' mercy, attempted to negotiate with one of the enemy commanders, Raymond of Toulouse. They chose him above others, as, apparently, he was a man of some mercy and of his word; in Jerusalem, it was Raymond who negotiated the surrender and safe passage, to Ascalon, of al-Dawla and his men, an act of moderation that brought Raymond much criticism from other crusading elements. At Ascalon, however, the crusaders did not extend their victory with the occupation of the city, and instead pulled back further north.

AL-AFDAL, AND THE TRAUMATIZED REMNANTS OF HIS ARMY, NOW RETREATED BACK TO THE CITY, WHERE THEY WERE EVACUATED FROM THE PORT BY NAVAL VESSELS.

Ascalon was just one of many battles, minor and major, that the crusaders would fight over the next half century, the period in which they consolidated what we today call the Crusader States, but which at the time were referred to collectively as Outremer, the 'land beyond the sea'. As we shall see in this chapter, the tapestry of life in this 1300km-long (800 mile) strip of territory presents a complex interweaving pattern. It was a time of both conflict and compromise, segregation and assimilation (to use two of the key terms in the historical interpretation of this era), tradition and innovation. In total, the age of the Crusader States would last for nearly 200 years, meaning that entire generations of Franks and other Europeans would be born, live and die in a culture very different from that of their family origins.

Below: A depiction of the battle of Ascalon, fought on 12 August 1099. Note the visible crosses, made from red cloth, identifying the crusaders.

THE CRUSADER STATES

When we speak of the Crusader States, we are specifically referring to four geo-political entities: the County of Edessa, the Principality of Antioch, the County of Tripoli and the Kingdom of Jerusalem. Each had its own set of rulers, a fact that often resulted in varying levels of friction between neighbouring states.

Above: The coronation of Baldwin I on Christmas Day 1100. Baldwin oversaw the dramatic geographical expansion of the Crusader States, and the building of key fortifications and settlements.

The County of Edessa

In the far north-east was the County of Edessa, as carved out independently by Baldwin. Straddling the Euphrates River, and with its capital Edessa located vulnerably on its far eastern border, the county was somewhat apart from the rest of the crusading states, culturally and politically, and did not always enjoy good relations with its immediate neighbour, the Principality of Antioch. The county was also pressed upon by powerful Muslim and Turkish forces, particularly those centred on the city of Mosul to the east (in what is today northern Iraq) and Aleppo (Syria) to the south. Baldwin of Edessa, its ruler, thereby found himself in a frequent state of conflict, sometimes with significant personal consequences. On 7 May 1104, for example, Edessa itself was besieged by a Seljuk Turkish force of men under Jikirmish of Mosul and Sokman of Mardin. In an effort to divert Seljuk attention away from the siege, Baldwin and Bohemund of Antioch themselves led out an army to besiege the city of Harran. This manoeuvre had its intended effect, but also led to a crusader defeat in battle around Harran, one in which Baldwin himself was taken prisoner during a Seljuk cavalry charge. Baldwin would only be freed from captivity in 1108, following the payment of a ransom. The clash at Harran was just one of many battles the County of Edessa would fight during the first half of the twelfth century, the eastern portion of the county in particular changing its boundaries due to Muslim penetrations. It was the fall of the city of Edessa in 1144 that helped to trigger the Second Crusade.

The Principality of Antioch

This state occupied a large swathe of territory in what is today south-eastern Turkey and western Syria. At the point of this establishment, the Principality of Antioch was solidly the domain of Bohemund, much to the antagonism of the Byzantines, who had expected Antioch to be returned to their fold after its capture. Like Baldwin, however, Bohemund was to spend time as a prisoner of the Muslims, following his capture at the battle of Melitene in August 1100. During this time the principality was ruled over by Bohemund's regent, his nephew Tancred, until

Below: At the battle of Ager Sanguinis, also known as the 'Battle of the Field of Blood', a crusader army under Roger of Salerno was vanquished by the Muslim army of Aleppo.

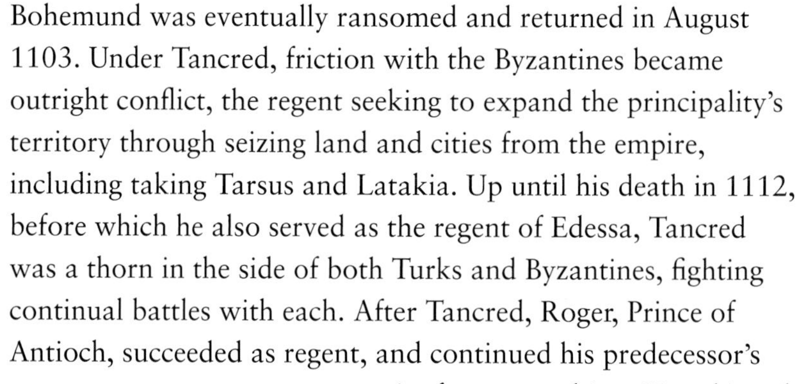

Bohemund was eventually ransomed and returned in August 1103. Under Tancred, friction with the Byzantines became outright conflict, the regent seeking to expand the principality's territory through seizing land and cities from the empire, including taking Tarsus and Latakia. Up until his death in 1112, before which he also served as the regent of Edessa, Tancred was a thorn in the side of both Turks and Byzantines, fighting continual battles with each. After Tancred, Roger, Prince of Antioch, succeeded as regent, and continued his predecessor's appetite for war-making. He achieved a major victory over the Seljuks at the battle of Danith on 14 September 1115, preventing Turkish attempts to reoccupy Syria, but on 27 June 1119 he was killed and his army destroyed by the forces of Ilghazi of Mardin (the ruler of Aleppo) at the 'Battle of the Field of Blood' near Aleppo; the lurid title of the battle was given because there were almost no Christian survivors – by this stage the Muslim forces were in no mood for mercy.

Below: The coronation of Baldwin II on 1118. Baldwin's reign was relatively successful, despite at one point being a prisoner of the Turks (1123-24).

Following Roger's death, Antioch subsequently became a vassal state of the Kingdom of Jerusalem, ruled over first by King Baldwin II then by a succession of regents who included Raymond of Poitiers from 1136 to 1149, who governed alongside the patriarch Ralph of Domfront. Raymond continued Antioch's now-established tradition of making war against the Byzantines, but Emperor John II Comnenus (r. 1118–43), after a protracted series of conflicts, eventually forced Raymond to pay homage to Constantinople. Raymond's end eventually came in 1149, when he was defeated at the battle of Inab. He was beheaded, and his head was given as a present to the caliph of Baghdad to be displayed in a silver box.

ALI IBN TAHIR AL-SULAMI (D. 1106)

From the Muslim perspective, Ali ibn Tahir al-Sulami of Damascus is a noteworthy philosophical figure in the early history of the Crusader States. A jurist and philologist by profession, al-Sulami was appalled by both the Christian expansion in the Middle East and by the lack of a unified Muslim response to that threat. In 1105 he wrote a treatise entitled *Kitab al-Jihad (Book of Holy War)* and presented it as a series of lectures in the Great Mosque in Damascus. There he not only explained some of the political realities behind the Crusades, but also demonstrated how Muslim disunity had opened the door to crusader success. In one passage from the book he stated: 'Their [the crusaders'] desires are multiplying all the time because of what appears to be the Muslims' abstinence from opposing them, and their hope so invigorated by virtue of what they see as their enemies' contentedness with being unharmed by them, until they have become convinced that the whole country will become theirs and all its people will be prisoners in their hands. May God in his generosity humble their ideas by bringing together everyone and arranging the unity of the people, for he is near, and answers prayers.' Although al-Sulami's ideas had a limited practical effect within the Muslim world at this time, his call for a co-operative military *jihad* was absorbed by many Muslim rulers and commanders, and would come to have increasing influence over time.

County of Tripoli

The County of Tripoli was the smallest of the four Crusader States, sandwiched between the Principality of Antioch to the north and the Kingdom of Jerusalem to the south. It was actually the last of the states to be formed, as Tripoli itself was not captured until 1109. The original ambition to take the city was held by Raymond of Toulouse, who had conducted an unsuccessful siege of Tripoli in 1105, just prior to his death on 25 February. After his death, the succession was contested between Count William Jordan of Cerdanya, a warrior who had continued the siege of Tripoli, and Raymond's late-arriving and possibly illegitimate son, Bertrand. It was Bertrand's contribution of a more powerful naval fleet, manned by sailors from Provencal and Genoa, that finally gave the crusaders the capability to take Tripoli.

Above: 'The Taking of Tripoli', 1109: Bertrand of Toulouse, the eldest son of Raymond of Tolouse, receives the surrender and obeisance of Fakhr al-Mulk, the Fatimid ruler of the city.

Following this victory, there was an attempt to resolve the brewing conflict between the two men by dividing the County of Tripoli between them, but first William and then Bertrand died in relatively close proximity, and in 1112 Bertrand's son Pons took control. Pons was not destined to be one of the Crusader States' most shining rulers. In his efforts to claim southern parts of the Tripolitan territory from the Kingdom of Jerusalem, he came into open conflict with both Baldwin II in 1122 and Fulk of Anjou in 1132. Suffering heavy defeats through his rebellions, and fighting new Shia 'Assassin' armies along the north-eastern border, Pons achieved little more than politically and militarily weakening the County of Tripoli for those who came after him. He was killed in battle in 1137 and Raymond II took over his diminished kingdom. Nevertheless, the County of Tripoli came to possess some of the most influential fortifications of the Crusader States, including the unrivalled Krac des Chevaliers (see below).

The Kingdom of Jerusalem

The Kingdom of Jerusalem was the spiritual centre of Outremer. Rule over this territory was at first offered to Raymond of Toulouse, but he rejected the proposition, stating that the title of 'king' over the Holy Land would be inappropriate – only Christ himself should hold that honour. Thus, Godfrey of Bouillon took the leadership under the evasively grandiloquent title of 'Defender of the Holy Sepulchre'.

Godfrey demonstrated some initiative in the early days of his rule – such as his army's victory at the battle of Ascalon – but also some political decisions that created disturbances within the nascent kingdom. He negotiated treaties with the Muslim rulers of Ascalon, Acre and Caesarea, actions that raised eyebrows among the more belligerent crusaders, who resisted anything that smacked of assimilation or accommodation. He also accepted

Below: The funeral of Godfrey of Bouillon in Jerusalem, 23 July 1100. Subsequently Godfrey was remembered by some as the 'perfect Christian knight'.

Above: The cache is a silent testimony to one of the most dramatic events in the history of Caesarea – the violent conquest of the city by the crusaders in 1101. Someone hid their fortune, hoping to retrieve it, but never returned.

the authority of the new Latin patriarch of Jerusalem, Dagobert of Pisa, who filled the gap left by the deposing of the first Latin Patriarch, Arnulf of Chocques, on the grounds of an uncanonical election. Yet both Godfrey and Dagobert's influence over the city would be short lived. Godfrey died in July 1100, and Dagobert held sway for six months until sidelined by the arrival of Baldwin of Edessa (Godfrey's brother) the following December. Baldwin compelled Dagobert to crown him king of Jerusalem, and within 12 months the patriarch was expelled from the city on charges of embezzlement, the authenticity of which are an open question.

Baldwin was undoubtedly the *primus inter pares* of all the rulers of the Crusader States. Unlike his now-deceased brother, Baldwin was focused on a more aggressive security policy for Outremer. An early priority was to capture the coastal ports that remained in Muslim hands. Arsuf and Caesarea were taken in 1101, the former largely without bloodshed after the sage surrender of the population, the latter destroyed after showing resistance, its population either killed or enslaved. In 1104 he conquered Acre, in cooperation with the Genoese fleet – Genoa would do well commercially through its support for Baldwin, being rewarded with special trading conditions and revenue collection zones within the newly acquired ports. By 1112 the only coastal cities that remained outside Baldwin's reach were Ascalon and Tyre. In addition to the coastal campaigns, he also fought Fatimid armies in the south and Seljuk armies in the north, not always victoriously but ultimately building a more secure and powerful kingdom.

Opposite: The death of Baldwin I, 2 April 1118. The king had requested that as his final moments approached, he be carried to the spot where Christ had risen from the dead.

In 1118 Baldwin died, succumbing to an old war wound while campaigning on the Nile. His cousin, Baldwin II (Baldwin

I died childless), inherited the kingdom and ruled over it until his own death in 1131, again fighting constant wars against a variety of enemies. Prior to his death, of natural causes, Baldwin II was much preoccupied with ensuring his succession. He had four daughters but no sons, and sought to make a supporting marriage alliance for his eldest daughter, Melisende. She was therefore married to Fulk, Count of Anjou, and in 1129 they went on to have a son, also called Baldwin. In an apparent effort to ensure that Fulk did not unilaterally take over the kingdom after Baldwin II's death, the king engineered the succession so that both Melisende and Fulk were crowned joint rulers of the Kingdom of Jerusalem, the coronation taking place on 14 September 1131.

From this awkward situation, one certainly not desired by Fulk, grew one of those royal intrigues so typical of the era. Summarizing broadly, Fulk attempted to sideline his wife, but she pushed back vigorously, aided by the youthful, handsome and warrior-like Hugh, Count of Jaffa. Suspicions about the relationship between Melisende and Hugh naturally flourished, and at one point Fulk had Hugh arrested, found guilty of high treason and sentenced to exile. Melisende had the sentence overturned, but after a subsequent attempt on Hugh's life by an assassin (likely sponsored by Fulk or his supporters), the queen was able to generate more support for her cause, and Fulk was compelled to comply with the original vision of joint rulership.

Opposite: This map shows the rather complex relationship between the Christian and Muslim states in the Middle East in the twelfth and thirteenth centuries, when the crusader states reached their greatest extent.

Below: King Fulk is haunted in his dream by the victims of his outrages, in this reimagining of psychological history.

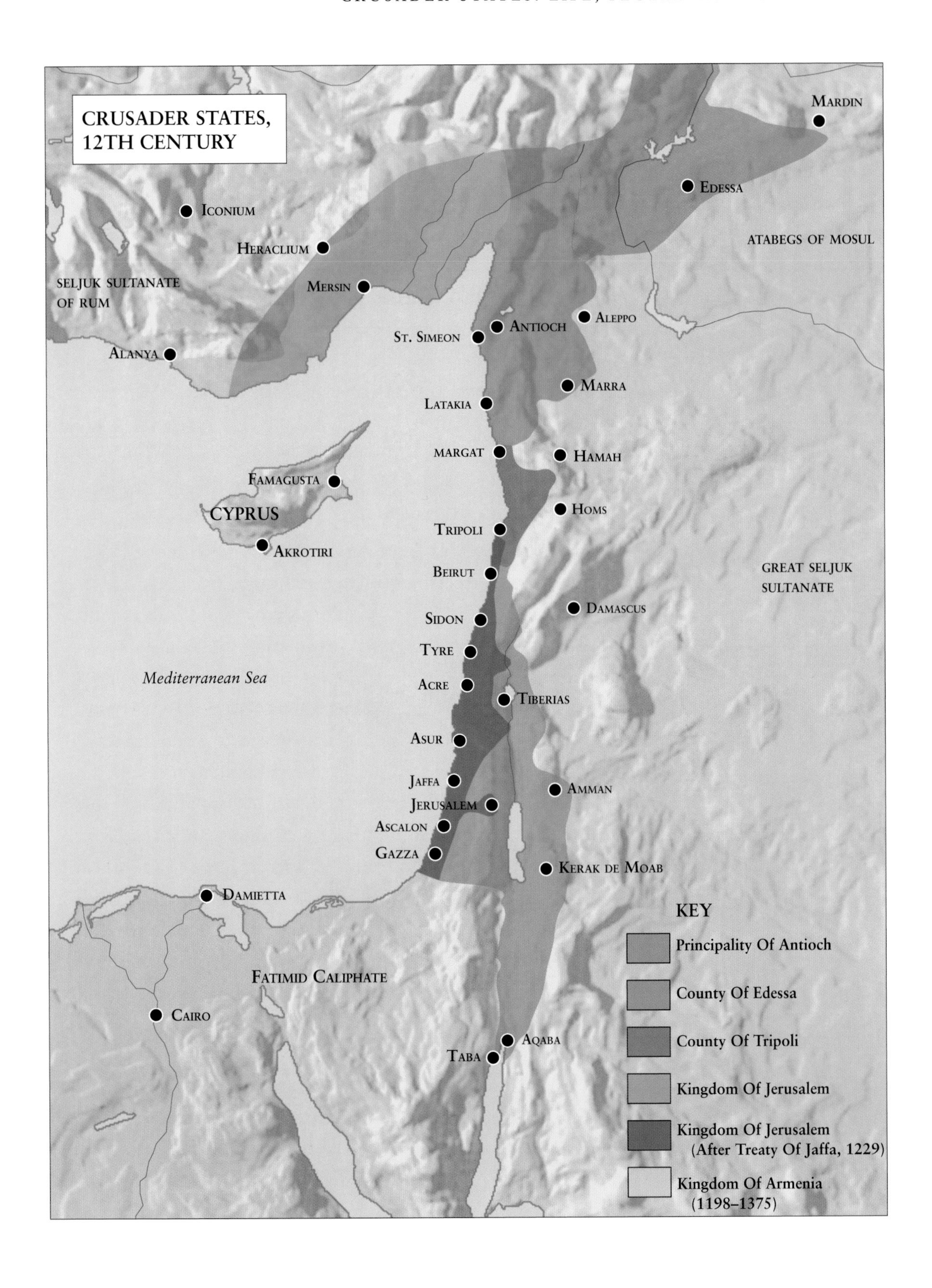
CRUSADER STATES, 12TH CENTURY
Mardin
Edessa
Atabegs of Mosul
Iconium
Heraclium
Seljuk Sultanate of Rum
Mersin
Aleppo
Antioch
St. Simeon
Alanya
Marra
Latakia
Margat
Hamah
Famagusta
Cyprus
Homs
Tripoli
Akrotiri
Beirut
Great Seljuk Sultanate
Damascus
Sidon
Tyre
Mediterranean Sea
Acre
Tiberias
Asur
Jaffa
Amman
Jerusalem
Ascalon
Gazza
Kerak de Moab
Damietta
KEY
Principality Of Antioch
County Of Edessa
County Of Tripoli
Kingdom Of Jerusalem
Kingdom Of Jerusalem (After Treaty Of Jaffa, 1229)
Kingdom Of Armenia (1198–1375)
Fatimid Caliphate
Cairo
Aqaba
Taba

OULTREJORDAIN

ALTHOUGH NOT ONE OF the Crusader States, Oultrejordain was an important part of the crusader world. It was a borderless and larger territory, extending out to the east of the Jordan River, and had been controlled by the Fatimids prior to the arrival of the First Crusade. In fact, it largely stayed in Muslim hands, the majority of the inhabitants being Shia Bedouin, but through the 'Lordship of Oultrejordain' it was regarded as a vassal of the Kingdom of Jerusalem. Several Christian strongholds were dotted throughout the territory, including Montreal, Kerak (Crac des Moabite) and Safed.

THE SETTLER ECONOMY

Following the victory at Jerusalem in 1099, many of the crusaders, now numbering only about 14,000, decided that they had had enough of campaign life in the Middle East and returned home to Europe, often considerably wealthier on account of Byzantine rewards and any plunder picked up along the way. But there was a significant portion who chose to stay on, and to build a new life a long way from their homelands. In addition, thousands of settlers migrated into Outremer, lured by its sunny promise. By the second half of the twelfth century, there were some 140,000 'Franks' (as they were known, actually incorporating a broad swathe of Europeans) settled in the Kingdom of Jerusalem, out of a total population of 650,000. Given the brittle nature of Crusader State politics, and the clear and present danger from surrounding Muslim peoples, what was in it for them?

BUT THERE WAS A SIGNIFICANT PORTION WHO CHOSE TO STAY ON, AND TO BUILD A NEW LIFE A LONG WAY FROM THEIR HOMELANDS.

Apart from the 'bulge' in the far north, formed by the Principality of Antioch and the County of Edessa, the Crusader States formed a very narrow strip of land hugging the Mediterranean coastline; at its narrowest point, around Tyre, it was scarcely 16km (10 miles) across. While the Middle Eastern interior was dominated by arid expanses, the coastal strip was extremely fertile, well-watered by the Orontes and Jordan Rivers that ran almost parallel to the coastline, punctuated by the Sea of Galilee in the south. Therefore, Outremer was an ideal place for flourishing agriculture, across a broad spectrum of crop types: wheat, barley, grapes, olives, figs, bananas, citrus fruits, vegetables and sugar cane. The rich soil conditions meant that many settlers experienced a variety in their diet that would have been almost inconceivable in many regions of Europe. To locally grown crops were added spices and other rare foodstuffs imported into the region via overland trade with central Asia and the Far East.

Naturally, the long Mediterranean coastline added to dietary diversity with the opportunities for intensive fishing, but through its numerous ports the settlers could also accrue wealth through trading their agricultural products overseas. A good example of this is the sugar cane industry, as the Crusader States became Western Europe's principal supplier of refined sugar, produced in huge royal sugar mills dotted throughout Palestine, although moved to Cyprus in the late thirteenth century to escape Muslim expansion.

Below: Montreal Castle, built in 1115 by Baldwin I of Jerusalem, was located on a hilltop in what is today Jordan. Its garrison policed trade routes between Egypt and Syria.

In addition to internal and international trade in agricultural products, the wealth of the Crusader States created and fostered a massive market for luxury goods, including jewellery (everything from religious items through to dress accessories), ceramics, glasswear, cutlery (metal forks were common in eastern culture, unlike in the west), bed linen, mosaics, decorative furniture and hanging carpets, such items typically produced with exquisite craftsmanship. The upshot of agricultural plenty and a vibrant trade in consumer goods was a rising level of personal wealth among all classes of settler. Indeed, pilgrims visiting Outremer from some of the dour reaches of Europe were frequently shocked at the levels of opulence, even within small rural settlements and domestic dwellings. The trade that resulted from crusader productivity also drove the rapid urban development of the major coastal ports. Italian and French traders in particular established major offices, warehouses and port facilities in places such as Tyre and Acre, streamlining the flow of goods between a productive East and a consuming West.

ITALIAN AND FRENCH TRADERS IN PARTICULAR ESTABLISHED MAJOR OFFICES, WAREHOUSES AND PORT FACILITIES IN PLACES SUCH AS TYRE AND ACRE.

CRUSADER SOCIETY

As in the West, crusader society was based upon a feudal model, with the sovereign at the top of the hierarchy and his authority cascading down through complex strata of nobles, lords, knights, mayors, magistrates, chamberlains and many others. As with all feudal societies, the system produced levels of wealth, from kings to peasants, yet in Outremer the grades of distinction between individuals were somewhat 'flatter' than in Western Europe – even isolated rural settlements seemed to enjoy a relative degree of opulence – and the nature of social authority differed in ways that for many visitors to the region seemed alarmingly non-traditional.

An important point to make straightaway is that Outremer was a true multicultural society, in which Christians, Jews, Muslims and some other faiths mixed relatively freely. When

Opposite: A scene of crusader warriors trading with local people in an opulent market. Traded goods were also imported through the Christian-held ports from as far afield as China and India.

IC XC
Ο ΕΥΑΓΓΕΛΙΣΤΗΣ ΜΑΤΘΑΙΟΣ
Ο ΕΥΑΓΓΕΛΙΣΤΗΣ ΙΩΑΝΝΗΣ

the crusaders first arrived, they noted how existing Christian settlers were almost visually indistinguishable from their Muslim neighbours, such were the levels of familiarity and interaction; the Christians had also long discovered the practicalities of Arab dress. Although crusader art from the subsequent centuries rarely indicates that the settlers adopted local dress, there are accounts of visitors spotting crusader knights wearing Arab headdress or other garments that were eminently sensible under the tropical sun.

MANY INTER-FAITH PERSONAL RELATIONSHIPS FLOURISHED FROM TRADING OR COMMERCIAL ACTIVITIES, OR OTHER CONTACTS.

'Blended co-existence' – to coin a rather awkward phrase – rather than outright integration seems to have defined the nature of relationships between the Frankish settlers and the Muslims. In the towns and cities, Muslim and Christian neighbourhoods would sit side-by-side. Out in the countryside, settlers built numerous pleasant villages, monasteries, farms, churches and manor houses, often a long way from the protection of castles or garrisons, their location indicating a certain degree of comfort in living surrounded by Muslim neighbours. Many inter-faith personal relationships flourished from trading or commercial activities, or other contacts.

Of course, there were some hard theological walls built between the faiths. In 1120, the Council of Nablus issued a series of 25 decrees concerned with matters of personal behaviour and social morality, including on sexual relations between Muslims and Christians. The twelfth decree, for example, stated that 'If anyone should be tried for having lain with a Saracen woman consensually, the Saracen women's nose should be cut off.' Similarly, 'If a Christian woman mixes with a Saracen by her own free will, let both be judged as having committed adultery. If in fact she was raped by him with force, she will not be held at fault, but the Saracen will be castrated.' It was clear from such rules that full assimilation was never to be permitted. Yet at the same time the decrees also make some attempt to define the rights of Muslims. The thirteenth decree states: 'If anyone should oppress [rape] his Saracen slave woman, she herself

Opposite: The Church of the Holy Sepulchre in Jerusalem is one of the most sacred sites in Christendom; its recapture was a central objective for the First Crusade.

Above: Knights and pilgrims celebrate Christmas in enraptured fashion in Bethlehem, at the site of Christ's birth. The city fell under Christian control in early June 1099.

will be marked and he himself will be castrated.' The following decree works in a similar vein: 'If anyone should push himself on a Saracen of another by force, he will undergo the sentence of an adulterer.' Clearly, the ethical balance here is still rather lopsided, but there does seem an implicit acknowledgement that the Muslim community is to be accorded a degree of respect. As these decrees were written at a time when militaristic crusading was still a prevailing spirit, such prohibitions might have been necessary to prevent naked displays of power.

Those who wrote the decrees should probably have been mindful of the fact that in many ways the Muslim culture was actually of greater sophistication than the one the crusaders had left behind. One of the most eloquent expositions of this truth comes from the pen of Usama ibn Munqidh, a warrior, diplomat, scholar and poet who interacted with the Frankish court at the highest levels. His work *Kitab al-I'tibar* (*Book of Contemplation*) reveals a unique Muslim perspective on the world of the Franks.

He makes the observation that, 'Those who have recently arrived from the Frankish lands have rougher character than those who have become acclimated and spent time in the company of Muslims.' To illustrate this, he recounts an incident when he visited the al-Aqsa Mosque. The mosque was by this time the headquarters for the Knights Templar, who counted among Usama ibn Munqidh's friends. They had converted a small church into a room in which he could pray. As he knelt to make his devotions, however, a newly arrived Frank rushed up to him, grabbed his head aggressively and turned his face towards the east, with the words: 'Pray like this!' Revealingly, some nearby Templars rushed to Usama ibn Munqidh's aid, grabbing the Frank and throwing him out, apparently keen to preserve inter-faith relations rather than protect the bullish attitudes of those who now appear as outsiders.

'THOSE WHO HAVE RECENTLY ARRIVED FROM THE FRANKISH LANDS HAVE ROUGHER CHARACTER THAN THOSE WHO HAVE BECOME ACCLIMATED AND SPENT TIME IN THE COMPANY OF MUSLIMS.'

As the twelfth century progressed, and the mentality of Outremer's new Christians shifted steadily from militarism to domesticity, Fulcher of Chartres observed that the mental distance between the settlers and their homelands grew ever greater:

> *Consider, I pray, and reflect how in our time God has transformed the Occident into the Orient.*
>
> 3. *For we who were Occidentals have now become Orientals. He who was a Roman or a Frank has in this land been made into a Galilean or a Palestinian. He who was of Rheims or Chartres has now become a citizen of Tyre or Antioch. We have already forgotten the places of our birth; already these are unknown to many of us or not mentioned any more.*
> 4. *Some already possess homes or households by inheritance. Some have*

Below: Pious crusader graffiti adorns the walls of the Church of the Holy Sepulchre. Such marks were a way of claiming the very fabric of the building for Christendom.

taken wives not only of their own people but Syrians or Armenians or even Saracens who have obtained the grace of baptism. One has his father-in-law as well as his daughter-in-law living with him, or his own child if not his stepson or stepfather. Out here there are grandchildren and great-grandchildren. Some tend vineyards, others till fields.

5. *People use the eloquence and idioms of diverse languages in conversing back and forth. Words of different languages have become common property known to each nationality, and mutual faith unites those who are ignorant of their descent. Indeed, it is written, 'The lion and the ox shall eat straw together' [Isaiah 62: 25]. He who was born a stranger is now as one born here; he who was born an alien has become as a native.*

This insightful passage not only explains how the crusaders adjusted to their new life, but also how divisions between outsiders and indigenous people began to break down. Settler marriages to Christian Syrians or Armenians, or even converted Muslims, brought an intermingling of cultures at the deepest levels. Nor was this phenomenon just seen amongst the crusading communities. In the Fatimid court, both Christians and Jews were often seen in significant positions within government, especially relating to administration and finance. Seen in this light, the idea of the Crusades as a brute 'us vs. them' scenario does not do justice to the subtleties of subsequent cultural adjustment.

WORDS OF DIFFERENT LANGUAGES HAVE BECOME COMMON PROPERTY KNOWN TO EACH NATIONALITY, AND MUTUAL FAITH UNITES THOSE WHO ARE IGNORANT OF THEIR DESCENT.

PILGRIMS AND WARRIORS

With the Holy Land now secure in Christian hands, pilgrims from Europe began to trace the steps of the crusaders as they made the long journey of faith. Although the First Crusade had brought victory, a pilgrimage was still a perilous undertaking, often passing through or near to regions still in the hands of

THE STATUS OF WOMEN

The Christian women of Outremer, generalizing beyond undoubted variations in personal circumstances, seem to have enjoyed a higher degree of both personal freedom and status than would have been deemed acceptable back in Europe. Women were no strangers to the throne in the Crusader States. We have already seen Melisende in this role, albeit a little contorted in relation to her husband, but there were other queens regnant during the crusader era, including Isabella I of Jerusalem (r. 1190–1205) and her young daughter Maria of Montferrat (r. 1205–1212). Women might also be found managing their husband's estates in their absence, and there were many notable instances of women even taking up the sword and riding out to battle (or organizing siege defences) alongside the menfolk. Examples of warrior women include Florine of Burgundy, Cecilia of Le Bourcq, Lady of Tarsus and Margaret of Provence. At a more domestic level, pilgrims to Outremer often remarked upon the way that local Christian women seemed to wander the streets and arrange their affairs more freely, and talked more confidently with members of the opposite sex, their husbands so familiar with this that they might occasionally leave their wives unaccompanied in the presence of a male friend. The wellspring of this openness could in part have been due to the simple fact that the large numbers of women who accompanied the First Crusade endured the same privations as the menfolk, often breeding a resourcefulness and resilience that couldn't be contained by mere convention.

Above: Florine of Burgundy was a French crusader, who led an army of about 1500 men alongside her husband, Sweyn the Crusader.

belligerent Turkish warlords. The dangers were brought home in a massive pilgrimage that embarked from Lombardy in September 1100, numbering in the many thousands, mostly armed civilians and with only a small group of soldiers to protect them. They reached Constantinople in March 1101, acquiring a body of Byzantine mercenaries before moving out into Anatolia. Interestingly, during this phase of the journey they were met by another pilgrimage led by Stephen of Blois, returning to the Holy Land with a cloud of shame still hanging over him. Near Amasya in northern Turkey, the huge crowd of now-exhausted pilgrims was ambushed by a rushing Turkish force, and 80 per cent of the entire Christian group was either killed or enslaved.

Above: Pilgrims reach the Holy Land, and raise their hands in thankfulness. Pilgrimage was often undertaken in contrition over former sins.

Of course, this event occurred only a very short time after the First Crusade, and tensions were still high, but, even so, pilgrims on subsequent journeys always remained potential prey from marauding gangs. It was in response to this situation that, in 1118, a group of noblemen made a proposition to King Baldwin, outlined here by medieval chronicler William of Tyre:

In this same year [1118], certain noble men of knightly rank, religious men, devoted to God and fearing him, bound themselves to Christ's service in the hands of the Lord Patriarch. They promised to live in perpetuity as regular canons, without possessions, under vows of chastity and obedience. Their foremost leaders were the venerable Hugh of Payens and Geoffrey of St Omer. Since they had no church nor any fixed abode, the king gave them for a time a dwelling place in the south wing of the palace, near the Lord's Temple. The canons of the Lord's Temple gave them, under certain conditions, a square near the palace which the canons possessed. This the knights used as a drill field. The Lord King and his noblemen and also the Lord Patriarch and the prelates of the church gave them benefices from their domains, some for a limited time and some in perpetuity. These were to provide the knights with food and clothing. Their primary duty, one which was enjoined upon them by the Lord Patriarch and the other bishops for the remission of sins, was that of protecting the roads and routes against the attacks of robbers and brigands. This they did especially in order to safeguard pilgrims.

Above: The French-Syrian historian William of Tyre was born into a settler family in c. 1130. He was highly cultured, speaking Latin, Greek, and Arabic.

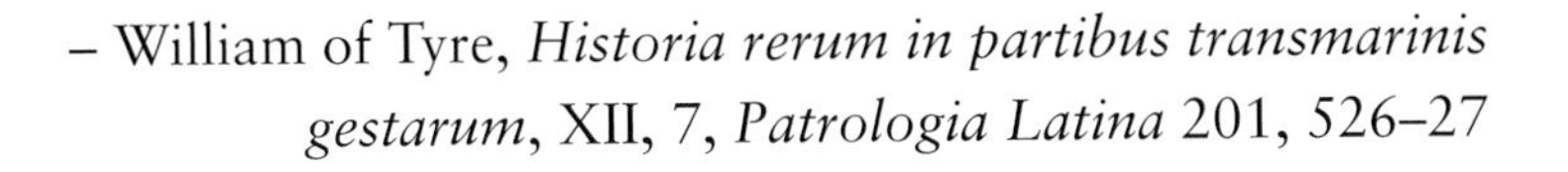

– William of Tyre, *Historia rerum in partibus transmarinis gestarum*, XII, 7, *Patrologia Latina* 201, 526–27

In this narrative, we read of the birth of the famous Order of the Knights Templar. These monastic warriors, known for their lifestyles of austerity, fanatical self-discipline and chastity, grew to be an organization of extraordinary power both within the Crusader States and across medieval Europe.

Headquartered in a wing of the royal palace in the al-Aqsa Mosque, the Order soon developed extensive landholdings and major commercial interests, and as their power grew they diversified into finance and banking. Soon, the influence of the Knights Templar would be relatively all-pervasive; some have argued that they constitute the world's first multinational corporation. Yet alongside their peaceful activities, they remained formidable warriors, fighting at the vanguard of some of the Crusades' most brutal battles.

The Knights Templar was not the only military order in Outremer, however. Another was the Knights Hospitallers, so called after the monks serving in the Hospital of St John in Jerusalem, one of the world's greatest medical centres at this time, with a capacity for 2000 patients and a professional (at least by the standards of the time) staff of doctors and nurses.

Below: A depiction of Knights Templar warriors standing before Jerusalem on the First Crusade. The full name of the order was the Poor Fellow-Soldiers of Christ and of the Temple of Solomon.

Despite their commitment to healthcare, the Hospitallers (or Knights of St John) also served as pious warriors, and like the Templars expanded their power enormously through acquiring land and money. Not only did they occupy entire quarters in the cities of Jerusalem and Acre, they were also responsible for building some of the finest crusader fortifications, including Krac des Chevaliers (see below). Another of the military orders was the Order of Brothers of the German House of Saint Mary in Jerusalem, more conveniently known as the Teutonic Order. Founded in c. 1190 in Acre, it controlled the port tolls there, but eventually moved out of Outremer for Eastern Europe in 1211.

At their height, the military orders would be an essential tool of administration of the Crusader States and a spearhead of further military actions. Power has a tendency to bring as many enemies as friends, however, and the Knights Templar in particular would become the target of persecution from King Philip IV of France in the early fourteenth century, and the Pope was forced to disband the Order.

ART AND ARCHITECTURE

Much of the portable art of the Crusader States has been lost to history, its elements scattered in the progressive collapse of Outremer over the twelfth and thirteenth centuries. Furthermore, defining what actually constitutes crusader art is complicated by the fact that the society of Outremer was so multicultural. In many cases, the individual pieces of art simply expressed the styles of their source community, with Syrian, Armenian, Byzantine, Turkish, Egyptian and Jewish influences all being expressed both individually and with varying degrees of intermingling between one another. There was also the extensive importation of luxury artistic objects from further afield, including from Central Asia, India and even East Asia (the crusaders were amongst the first European-born users of Chinese porcelain, for example). Further subdividing the spectrum of genres and objects is the overlaying distinction between religious and secular art. What we can at least say is that Frankish society certainly placed a high value upon artistic objects, whether for domestic consumption or trade, or for the expression of religious rites.

Certain types of artistic objects proliferated within Outremer, especially glazed ceramic tableware, ornate jewellery in silver and mother-of-pearl – often adorned with coloured precious stones – and glass vases and drinking vessels produced in major manufacturing centres in Tyre, Beirut and Antioch. Incidentally, the use of glass in the Crusader States seems far more extensive in this period than in Europe, not least in the fitting of glass windows to domestic housing.

Below: This detail from the west stained glass window, Church of St Andrew, Temple Grafton, Warwickshire, shows a Knights Hospitaller, the mark of the cross proudly adorning his cloak.

THE CRUSADER STATES WERE A TRUE MELTING POT OF CULTURES, AND WORK ON THE GREAT BUILDINGS WOULD INVOLVE INDIVIDUALS WHO LEARNED THEIR CRAFT IN WESTERN OR EASTERN EUROPE...

In terms of artistic styles in Outremer, there is an identifiable fusion of East and West in the religious art and architecture, the Western traditions of iconography and figurative art blended with the geometrical floral patterns seen in Islamic art (commonly known as arabesque). We see such syncretism, for example, in the famous psalter (prayer book) presented by an apparently penitent (or at least humbled) Fulk to Melisende in 1135; the back cover features scenes of a king (likely Fulk himself) performing good deeds, these scenes wrapped in perfect arabesque swirls. Similar patterns can be identified in the Church of the Holy Sepulchre, a beautiful vaulted building in which multiple influences appear to the fore. Such is not surprising. The Crusader States were a true melting pot of cultures, and work on the great buildings would involve individuals who learned their craft in Western or Eastern Europe but then worked under the instruction of new masters. For example, a Byzantine sculptor or fresco painter might have to adapt his work for a Western outlook, particularly in terms of subject matter, but the Eastern influence behind his work would still shine through. Byzantine-style mosaics are also a key ingredient of many religious buildings; in many ways, it seems that the settlers brought Western features of structural architecture, such as the ribbed vault, while the decorative elements were frequently indebted to Byzantine artistry and, on occasion, Islamic inspiration.

Below: A Byzantine cross with an engraving of St Stephen. Many such high-quality religious objects were brought back from the Levant by the crusaders.

The domestic housing of the Crusader States was typically stone- or brick-built (timber was not as plentiful in the Middle East as it was in Europe), with wall surfaces either plastered or faced in marble. The houses tended to be one to three stories high (additional floor space was given via a roof-top terrace), connected by external stairways, and an architectural style dominated by simple arches, arched or square windows divided by stonework, and, in wealthier housing, arcades and pillars. Courtyards, shaded by awnings or vine arbours, or gardens (for those with land) provided cool outdoor spaces; the courtyards were either private or, in poorer communities, shared with other houses. The main working space of the house was the kitchen, although if the dwelling was also a place of working-class trade, such as a shop or workshop, a door in the house front could be opened up to direct street access. Water was stored in cisterns or wells, and guttering from the roof channelled any precious rainwater into these vessels.

Above: The ivory back cover of Queen Melisende's Psalter was a carving of exquisite detail. Inside the book were 24 colour illuminations of New Testament scenes.

FORTIFICATIONS

Historically, the crusaders are less well known for their domestic architecture as they are for their fortifications. 'Crusader castles' is a blanket term for what was in reality a body of architectural work of many different forms and functions. While castles were certainly built for defensive purposes, they would equally be used as centres of administration, trade and even worship. The plurality of functions often explains the fact that not all crusader castles were logically located in places under military threat, especially in the first 70 years of the Crusader States, a time of greater stability. Only in the latter part of the twelfth century and during the thirteenth century were new castles built for defence/offence against outsiders, especially on the eastern face of the kingdoms, although they still retained their important administrative roles.

The scale, location and design of the crusader castles varied enormously. There were real monsters, some of the largest and

Above: Located near Baniyas, Syria, Margat Castle was one of the most impressive of the crusader fortifications, sat on an extinct volcano 360m (1181ft) above sea level.

most formidable examples of fortress building in the world, from physically elevated and relatively isolated bastions such as Krac des Chevaliers, Saone, Le Vaux Moix and Margat, to castles dominating urban centres, examples being Caesarea Maritima and Arsuf. There were also numerous minor fortifications dotted far and wide. Castel Blanc at Safita (southern Syria), for example, was essentially a large stone keep doubling as both a chapel and a fortress, built by the Knights Templar, and fortified way-stations and manor houses formed defensive outposts in many rural territories. Together, they formed a highly visible power projection, and potential breakwaters against invasions from outside.

The crusaders, and the settlers who made their lives in Outremer, established a way of life that was recognizably connected to the lands from which they hailed, but which also, over time, became a culture in its own right. Neither entirely separate from nor fully assimilated into the surrounding Muslim world, it attempted to strike a balance between the faiths that held the possibility of being sustainable. As the next chapter shows, however, such a hope was a fragile one indeed.

KRAC DES CHEVALIERS

SAT 650M (2130ft) on a hill east of Tartus, Syria, the great Krac des Chevaliers was primarily built between 1142 and 1170 by the Hospitallers, although the location was already the site of an earlier Kurdish fortress. It is a huge fortress, one that continued in development throughout the thirteenth century. A long outer curtain wall stood 9m (30ft) high and 3m (10ft) thick, divided up by 13 towers. The inner ward was dominated by a steep 30m (100ft) wide glacis or talus (sloped embankment), itself punctuated at the top by crenellated towers, bastions and walls. Despite its defendable limestone bulk, however, the castle was also a place of worship and administration, featuring a chapel, beautiful ribbed vaults, the Hall of the Knights, plus accommodation for about 60 men in garrison. The castle has survived to this day and remains imposing, although tragically it has been damaged during fighting in the Syrian civil war that began in 2011.

Below: Krac des Chevaliers still has the power to impress, nearly nine centuries after it was originally constructed. Note the steep glacis rising up off the outer wall.

3

THE SECOND CRUSADE AND THE RISE OF SALADIN

The Second Crusade (1147–49) was a disaster of a magnitude equal to the success of the First Crusade. Not only did the Frankish armies suffer catastrophic and humiliating defeats, they also helped lay the groundwork for the resurgence of Muslim power over the Crusader States.

By THE 1140s, the Crusader States – four decades old – were beginning to project something of a sense of divinely appointed permanence. It was an illusion. To the north and especially to the east, there remained the threat of the Muslim expansion, demonstrated by intermittent localized conflict. The principal centres of Muslim power to the east were the great cities of Mosul and Aleppo, ruled by Zangi Imad al-Din, a man known for a fearsome cruelty combined with a disorientating capricious nature – one of his disincentives for desertion was to cut two men in half for every one that deserted – but also for his skilful generalship. Further south, Damascus,

Opposite: King Louis VII takes the cross at Saint-Denis. One of Louis' greatest challenges for the Second Crusade was raising the requisite funds to create and to sustain the campaign.

under Emir Unur, was also a Muslim stronghold, albeit one that had made a pragmatic accommodation with the Franks; at this point in time, Unur feared Zangi more than the European settlers. In the far south, of course, was the Fatimid kingdom of Egypt which again, despite periodic fractures in relations, had largely adjusted itself to the presence of the Crusader States.

ANY COMPLACENCY FELT BY OUTREMER'S INHABITANTS WAS SHATTERED IN NOVEMBER 1144, WHEN ZANGI'S ARMIES SUDDENLY ATTACKED THE CITY OF EDESSA.

Any complacency felt by Outremer's inhabitants was shattered in November 1144, when Zangi's armies suddenly attacked the city of Edessa, taking advantage of the absence of Joscelin II (the city's ruler) and his forces. Edessa was locked in a siege for more than a month, and its walls were finally brought down on 24 December, precipitating the now almost customary massacre of many of its inhabitants.

Zangi's attack was not without logic. Joscelin II had made a pact with one of Zangi's Seljuk rivals, a pact that Zangi had now shattered. But for the Franks, this advance was an ominous portent. It not only destabilized the northern 'buffer zone' (as we might call it) between the Crusader States and the Seljuk Turks, it also confronted them with a potential direct threat to their long-term survival. Something had to be done.

Below: Pope Eugenius III was a pious and largely respected man, although the failure of the Second Crusade undermined his authority with many nobles.

A NEW ARMY

This time, it was the states of Outremer themselves who made a direct appeal to the Pope, Eugenius III, to raise another crusading army to push back the Muslim threat. Eugenius readily bought into the idea of the Second Crusade, and on 1 December 1145 issued his bull *Quantum praedecessores* enjoining Europe to commit itself again to a holy war. This time, however, he had a royal participation directly in his sights, specifically that of King Louis VII of France and the German king Conrad III of Hohenstaufen, 'King of the Romans'.

Actually, by the time the *Quantum praedecessores* arrived with Louis, the French monarch was likely already formulating plans for his own crusade. During a two-year conflict with the Comte de Champagne, Theobald II, Louis had a very direct and personal involvement in several atrocities, including the burning of a church in the town of Vitry-le-François with 1500 people inside it. Later, struck with guilt, and doubtless therefore attracted to the remission of sins promised in the *Quantum praedecessores*, Louis signed up readily to the papal crusade, despite the concerns of his chief minister, Abbot Suger of St Denis, that the military campaign would ruin the state finances. Suger was nevertheless appointed regent over France during his king's absence, Louis appreciating a safe pair of hands.

Below: Louis VII pulls back from the burning church at Vitry-le-François, torched on his orders. His guilt over this act, plus condemnation from the Church, gave him moral motivation to join the Crusades.

ELEANOR OF AQUITAINE

Above: The marriage of Eleanor of Aquitaine (left) and Louis VII of France (1137), left, and their subsequent embarkation on the Second Crusade.

AT THE TIME OF the Second Crusade, Louis VII was married to Eleanor of Aquitaine, a woman of abundant dynastic landholdings in Western Europe, who was also known for her outstanding beauty, high spirits and intelligence. Alongside her husband, Eleanor also took up the cross in March 1146, alongside many members of her female retinue. Her decision was doubtless aided by the close relationship she held with her uncle, Raymond of Antioch; rumours would even swirl that the two had an incestuous and adulterous relationship. Some historians have suggested that the female crusading cohort even dressed up fearsomely as Amazons, although this interpretation has been contested. Nevertheless, Eleanor marched with the crusaders, often in the van of the forces, although the actual combat contribution of her entourage was limited, and even criticized. Eleanor and her husband managed to survive the subsequent military disasters in Anatolia, yet their relationship suffered a fatal blow at Antioch, when Louis forcibly dragged Eleanor out on a campaign against Jerusalem; Eleanor had argued, with justification, that Raymond's alternative campaign against Muslim Aleppo was the more strategically sound. In 1152, her marriage to Louis was annulled, and she thereafter married Henry II of England. The marital attachment of her vast landholdings in France to the English king was a major factor in the later onset of the Hundred Years' War (1337–1453).

Louis VII's enthusiasm for the Crusade was not, at first, matched by many of his nobles and citizenry. To galvanize public support, Pope Eugenius II deployed the considerable oratorical, scriptural and psychological skills of the Cistercian monk Bernard of Clairvaux. Bernard began a pounding public relations drive around Europe, his first major stop being a large-scale recruitment event on 31 March 1146, in the presence of King Louis, at Vézélay in northern Burgundy. Conducted from a wooden stage in a large field next to the church, the event was a roaring success, thousands of people flocking to join the new Crusade; a vast pile of fabric crosses had been prepared in readiness. Louis himself lay before Bernard, weeping and anguished in penitence, before being raised to his feet and taking up the cross. His wife, Eleanor of Aquitaine, also theatrically joined him on the quest.

Below: Saint Bernard preaches the Second Crusade at Vézélay in Burgundy. His powers of oratory led many hundreds of people to take up the cross.

Following Vézélay, Bernard and other church representatives continued onwards, preaching across France and Germany. A key objective was the recruitment of Conrad III. Conrad was already a papal ally, having assisted the church in countering Norman campaigns in Italy. He had also made a visit to the Holy Land in 1124. He was nevertheless initially more resistant to calls to join the Crusade. Bernard presented the case for war to Conrad in Frankfurt in November 1146; at this time, Conrad

Above: Conrad III taking the cross. Monarchical commitment to a Crusade was always a risky business, involving long periods away from scheming courts.

Opposite: This Sicilian church mosaic shows Christ himself presiding over the coronation of the king of the Normans, Roger II.

was embroiled in civil conflict with other restless German rulers. But once these issues were somewhat resolved, partly through Bernard's negotiations, Conrad recognized the opportunity to increase his prestige and status, plus succumbed to some moral blackmail, and committed himself to the campaign.

TENSIONS

For the Second Crusade, there would also be a broader internationalism in the composition of forces. Preaching in England, for example, brought a large number of recruits, many of them incentivized by a desire to escape endemic civil conflict and the persecution delivered by Norman-French overlords. The crusade also included the forces of Roger II of Sicily, who by this time had risen to become king not only of Sicily but most of

ΡΟΓЄΡΙΟϹ ΡΗΞ
ΙϹ

southern Italy. This ascent had brought him into direct conflict with the papacy, many other Frankish states and the Byzantine Empire. Indeed, the emperor, Manuel I, was both aggrieved and suspicious that the new crusading army would include Roger; there were not-unreasonable fears that at least part of the crusading force could be easily redirected from fighting the Muslims to fighting the Byzantines. There was also the possibility that the French could ally with Roger in a concerted campaign against the Byzantine Empire. It was for this reason that Manuel, avoiding a potential war on two fronts, would actually make a temporary peace treaty with the Seljuks in the autumn of 1147, a decision later used to accuse him of all manner of perfidy.

Below: Amalric of Jerusalem (kneeling) pays homage to Emperor Manuel I, hoping for Byzantine help in defending Outremer.

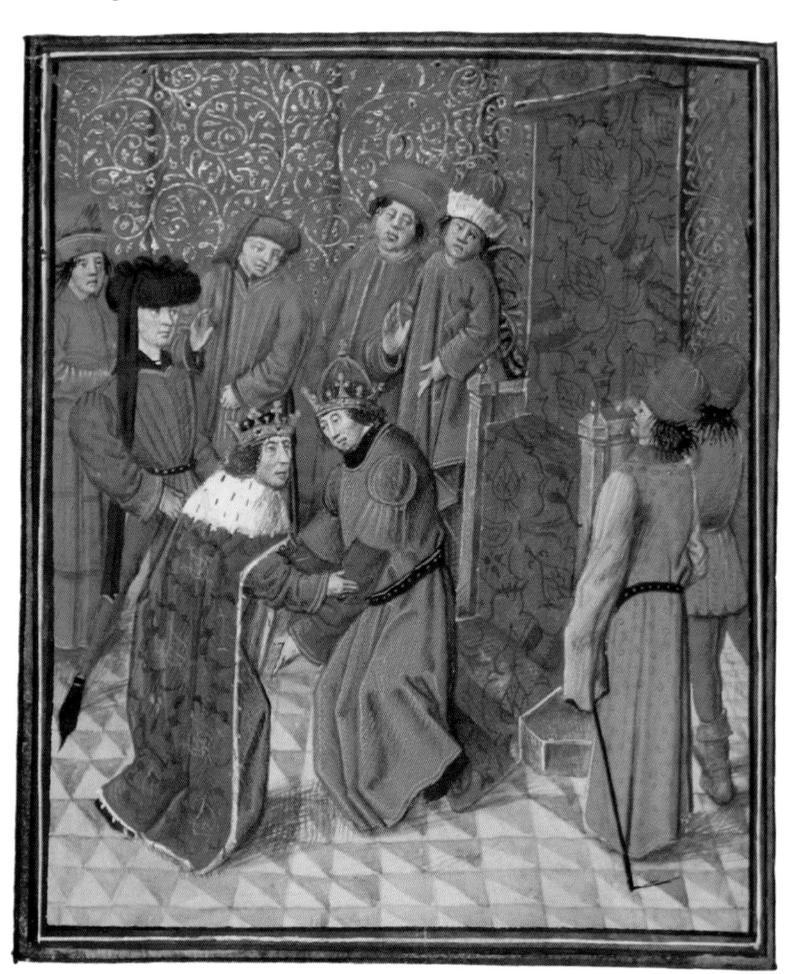

The situation with Roger was but one of the creaking floorboards under the feet of the Second Crusade. The Crusade had no explicit objectives stated in the *Quantum praedecessores*, not even the recapture of Edessa. In essence, the only concern of the crusaders was to turn up and fight the infidel; combined with a split leadership – no one was specifically 'in charge' – here was a recipe with disastrous consequences.

Regarding the army itself, its composition was heavily weighted towards non-combatant civilians, a situation that Eugenius had specifically, and unsuccessfully, tried to avoid. Unlike the First Crusade, the Second Crusade was launched towards already established

Crusader States, which dangled the prospect of a new life for all sorts of people, not all of them desirable individuals or prepared for the hardships of campaign life. Sources indicate that they even included criminals seeking a quick route to escape the authorities or justice.

Above: Bernard of Clairvaux defends German Jews during the Second Crusade. He declared that 'The Jews are not to be persecuted, killed, or even put to flight.'

One of the salient issues of the Second Crusade, as with all of the Crusades, was bringing discipline to a body of people easily given to violent opportunism and religious fanaticism, and who also frequently saw the societies and landscapes either side of the pilgrims' road as basically larders to be plundered. One way to control the latter instinct was for the monarchs and lords to ensure that ample supplies travelled with the forces. This was problematic, however, on account of factors such as primitive logistics and poor harvests. It was for this reason, and because of the occasional brutalities visited by the crusaders upon local peoples, that the emperor would introduce what was in effect an armed guard while the crusaders were crossing Byzantine territory. Rulers like Conrad had sworn an oath of peace and fealty to Manuel, but Manuel rightly regarded this with arm's-length scepticism, not least because Conrad's army included firebrands such as Frederick, Duke of Swabia, who mistrusted anything that smacked of subservience to the Byzantines. Campaign logistics and pay could drain royal finances with frightening speed, so both Conrad and Louis were forced to impose new levies on their towns and churches.

RELIGIOUS FANATICISM, AND THE CRUDE DESIRE TO MAKE AN EARLY START ON THE BLOODLETTING, REARED ITS UGLY HEAD, AS IT HAD DONE IN THE EARLIER SO-CALLED PEOPLE'S CRUSADE.

Religious fanaticism, and the crude desire to make an early start on the bloodletting, reared its ugly head, as it had done in the earlier so-called People's Crusade. Even as the Crusade was being preached, impulsive violence against Jewish populations again took place. One particularly unpleasant leader of the pogroms was the French Cistercian monk Radulphe, who attacked Jewish communities in the Rhine Valley, murdering hundreds. Only the strongest protestations of Bernard of Clairvaux eventually, reluctantly, restrained him, although there were further outbreaks of anti-Semitic violence in pockets throughout France and Germany.

Once on the road, the crusaders were also something of a powder keg, triggered especially by the killings that seemingly inevitably happened as they passed through volatile territories. When a German crusader was murdered near Adrianople, for example, Frederick's merciless response was to sack a local monastery and slaughter 150 of its monks. These were brutal days indeed, and the tendency to impulsive violent action was one of just many factors that undermined the Second Crusade.

WHEN A GERMAN CRUSADER WAS MURDERED NEAR ADRIANOPLE, FOR EXAMPLE, FREDERICK'S MERCILESS RESPONSE WAS TO SACK A LOCAL MONASTERY AND SLAUGHTER 150 OF ITS MONKS.

THE FIRST DEFEATS

While some elements of the Second Crusade diverted their efforts to other theatres, notably the Iberian Peninsula and far northern Europe (see Chapter 5), the bulk of the army was destined for the Holy Land. As always, defining accurate manpower figures among all the exaggeration (Manuel estimated some 900,000 crusaders) is difficult, but there were likely about 20,000 Germans and 15,000 French. On top of this, once in Outremer the crusaders could expect their ranks to be expanded by the now-indigenous settler armies. Just as in continental Europe, Outremer retained feudal obligations, and all vassals owed the king a year of military service within the kingdom, payment only coming for additional time under arms.

The German contingent set off on their long overland march in May 1147, the French following in June, the Crusade's armies again split, with the intention of easing the logistical burden on the lands through which they passed. The journey down to Constantinople – the intended destination before the strike into Anatolia and the Holy Land – was its usual bad-tempered, ill-disciplined, hungry and periodically violent affair. Nevertheless, the Germans finally converged on the Byzantine capital in September, the French arriving one month later. Manuel, fearful of the recent arrivals, made them camp outside the city walls, furthering the bad feeling already present between the crusaders and the Byzantines.

Above: Turks attack a crusader column during the Second Crusade. European armies often struggled to fight in close terrain, preferring open battlefields.

It was at this point that the split command between Louis and Conrad showed itself. Despite their common goal, the French and the Germans would essentially divide and take different routes through Anatolia. Conrad would go directly south-east, heading towards Dorylaeum and Iconium, the same route taken by the First Crusade. This was directly against Manuel's advice; he advocated the longer but safer route following the coastline, which put distance between the march and the Turkish-controlled territory further east. This more judicious route would be the one taken by the French. Mindful of some of the risks, however, Conrad directed much of the baggage train and civilian pilgrims to take the coastal route, under the leadership of his half-brother, Otto of Freising. Yet given the natural human tendency to gravitate towards the familiar, many of this group marched out instead with the warriors.

Having crossed the Bosphorus, the Germans advanced down to Nicaea, which they left on 25 October and headed south-east. The Turks of the Sultanate of Rum knew that they were coming, preparing their defences in advance. In particular, they organized their armies into the highly mobile columns that could prey on a large, slow-moving body of crusaders, deploying these columns in wait at locations in which the foreigner could be trapped or channelled.

It was a disaster in the making. Within a week the crusaders were beginning to run out of food and water, the situation made worse by the barren larder presented by the countryside around and beyond Dorylaeum. Taking advantage of the enemy's weakened state, the Turks now launched an endless succession of cavalry raids, each sweep of the horses, each release of the bow, carrying away lives. The crusaders could do little to counter such tactics. Effective foraging became impossible, and on 25 October the Turks unleashed a major attack, one that killed or captured thousands of German warriors and citizens. On 26 October, Conrad's harried nobles argued for a retreat. A humiliated Conrad complied, and the German Crusade turned back for Nicaea, harassed brutally all the way by the Seljuks. Conrad himself suffered a head wound and became seriously ill.

Below: Louis VII (left centre) fights for his life during the battle of Mount Cadmus on 6 January 1148, the remnants of his bodyguard surrounding his horse.

The surviving elements of the German force finally reached Nicaea and relative safety. The French by this time had also crossed the Bosphorus, and were moving south along the Anatolian coast road; the Germans agreed to rendezvous with them at Lopardium, to the west of Nicaea, and march together. Conrad went part of the way with the French, reaching Ephesus, but then, at the invitation of the emperor, retired to Constantinople to recover from his injuries and sickness.

THE TURKS UNLEASHED THEIR ATTACK WITHOUT MERCY. THOUSANDS OF THEM WERE POSITIONED AMONG THE SURROUNDING ROCKS AND TREES, POURING PRECISION ARCHERY FIRE INTO THE ENEMY RANKS.

The march of the huge French column – it was reputedly more than 10km (6 miles) long – was an ordeal of endurance. The winter weather, which included drenching rainfall and snow, left the crusaders demoralized. At Ephesus, Louis had decided to increase the speed of the march by cutting directly east towards the port of Adalia, from where his army could be shipped across the Mediterranean to Outremer. It was a fateful decision, as the route took them through mountainous areas that were perfectly suited to the Seljuk style of warfare.

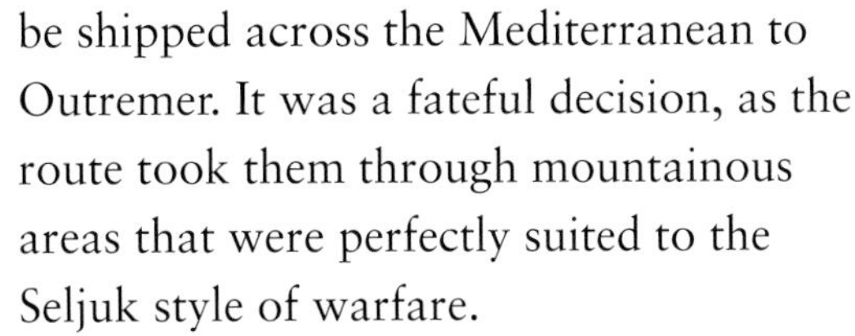

At the end of the first week of January 1148, the French had to cross Mount Cadmus via the Kazik Belli Pass. Not only did the pass rise to a precipitous 1250m (4101ft), but it also thinned the crusader column and took it through terrain ideally suited to Turkish ambush.

The Turks unleashed their attack without mercy. Thousands of them were positioned among the surrounding rocks and trees, pouring precision archery fire into the enemy ranks, and launching fast-moving raids down onto vulnerable sectors of the column. Many of the crusaders were backed off sheer drops,

CRUSADER ARMOUR

Left: A mail hauberk, similar to the type worn by the crusaders. Mail offered the advantage of dense metal protection, but with full articulation and freedom of movement.

FOR CRUSADER WARRIORS OF financial means (e.g. knights and nobles), the core piece of body armour was the hauberk, a knee-length mail coat. The tightly configured metal rings provided good protection against angular arrow and spear strikes (high-power hits at a right angle could force the links apart) and sword cuts, plus were flexible and relatively light – a standard short-sleeved suit (the most popular design) would weigh in the region of 5–9kg (11–20lb) depending on the means of construction. Later in the Crusades it became relatively common for warriors to extend the protection through sleeves that extended to the wrist. Legs were shielded by mail hose, worn over cloth trousers, the mail being tied just below the knee to prevent the hose slapping around too much under movement. Head protection came courtesy of a mail coif, either separate or incorporated directly into the hauberk, worn over a leather hat for comfort. There were also a variety of helmets, the designs often reflecting the country of origin, but the classic 'pot' style helmet with nose bar was particularly common from about the middle of the twelfth century. Altogether, the entire mail outfit could weigh in the region of 15kg (33lb), a not inconsiderable burden, especially under the Middle Eastern sun, which would heat the links to burning temperature. During the thirteenth century, crusaders often reinforced their armour, typically by donning a *gambeson* – a thick padded cloth coat that in itself could be capable of stopping an arrow (for the lower orders, this was their main form of battlefield armour) – or panels of thick boiled leather or metal plate.

falling to their deaths. Nevertheless, through the professionalism of some of his more seasoned warriors, and the advice of veteran Templars, Louis' army managed to avoid complete destruction, although the losses were appalling. His much-depleted force pressed on, and eventually reached Adalia around 20 January.

THE BATTLE OF DAMASCUS

From Adalia, the battle-weary French eventually sailed for their next destination, Antioch. The king, still accompanied by his wife Eleanor, arrived there in mid-March, to an opulent welcome by Raymond. It was at Antioch that the intricacies of court politics and strategic debate, plus the problematic relationship between Louis and Eleanor, progressively guided the Second Crusade towards its ultimate disaster.

As the crusaders planned their next move, in sketchy consultation with Raymond, Joscelin (he was currently residing in Antioch in exile) and others, a heated division of opinion emerged. This split became wide and visible at a major conference held in Acre, with all the powers of Outremer present, including King Baldwin III of Jerusalem. Neither side advocated the recapture of Edessa, a city that was now pretty much in ruins anyway. Raymond instead advocated a powerful campaign east to take Aleppo and Shaizar, thereby smashing Nur al-Din's power and ensuring the security of both Antioch and broader Outremer. This proposed campaign in northern Syria would also enable Raymond to secure more territory at the expense of the Byzantine Empire, although there was the possibility that Manuel would claim such territories for himself.

Below: Prince Raymond of Antioch welcomes the war-weary King Louis in March 1148. Relations between the two men would be fraught and suspicious.

Above: The Council of Acre (top), held in the summer of 1148, led to the ultimately disastrous decision to besiege Damascus (bottom).

Historians have found much to recommend Raymond's proposition, particularly from the point of view of ensuring future security for Outremer's eastern border. Politically, however, Louis and Baldwin exceeded Raymond in both power and status, and they had other plans. Instead they chose a southern drive on Damascus. Damascus had greater resonance in Christian history than Aleppo, but there were also some pragmatic arguments for the Damascene assault, not least that German forces under Conrad had redeployed by ship to Acre, and were therefore well-positioned to support the campaign. Yet historically, Emir Unur of Damascus had generally sought peaceable relations with the Franks, although the marriage of his daughter to Nur al-Din in 1147 had raised tensions somewhat. Nevertheless, Unur's instincts for peace could have been exploited by the Franks better; by attacking him, they made sure that he would become their enemy.

Yet Damascus it was. Eleanor vocally sided with her uncle, producing an explosive row between Eleanor and her husband that ended with Louis physically dragging her from Raymond's palace and consigning her to the march east. In mid-July, both the crusader army and the army of the Kingdom of Jerusalem had gathered in the city of Tiberius, about 110km (68 miles) southwest of Damascus, and then began their march towards their objective, heading through the upper Jordan Valley.

HISTORICALLY, EMIR UNUR OF DAMASCUS HAD GENERALLY SOUGHT PEACEABLE RELATIONS WITH THE FRANKS.

For the crusaders, Damascus was a complex prospect tactically. It was surrounded by a dense belt of orchards, with trees, mud walls, irrigation channels and numerous small watchtowers breaking up the landscape, to a distance of 8km (5 miles) from the city walls. The only advantage of this terrain for the attackers was that it was well watered, with the Barada River flowing towards and around the city on an east–west axis. Unur, well aware that the crusaders were heading his way, mobilized both his army and his citizens, preparing defensive positions within the orchards and blocking the city streets with rubble and other barricades.

Around 21 July, the crusading force began its penetration of the orchards. The going was tough. The Muslim troops launched incessant close-range ambushes with spears and bows; the fighting became more akin to counterinsurgency than open battlefield combat. Yet although Unur's men inflicted heavy casualties upon the enemy, numerical superiority enabled the Franks to push through the wooded barrier and reach the river and the city walls by 24 July.

For the next two days, ferocious fighting ensued, as Unur led an unrelenting defence of his walls. There was even a major Muslim counter-attack north of the Barada; it was unsuccessful, and simply added to Unur's ever-growing casualty list. It indeed looked as if Damascus might fall. Through those unpredictable shifts of fortune that accompany warfare, however, Damascus was saved by both Muslim intervention and crusader mistakes.

Faltering Strategy

As matters became more fraught inside the city, Unur had sent out messages – cries for help – to Nur al-Din, who promptly gathered a large army and despatched it south. Sayf al-Din (eldest son of Zangi; Nur al-Din was the younger son) of Mosul was also sending troops. At the same time, on 27 July the Frankish leadership, frustrated at their escalating casualties and a resilient enemy defence, decided to move their forces out to the more open, but also more barren and dry, area to the east of the city, which they felt was better for launching a direct assault. In fact, once out of the shade of the orchards, the crusaders and their horses simply baked uncomfortably in the sun, and in front of defences that proved just as strong as the opposite side of the city. Furthermore, they now learned that a massive Muslim relief army was on its way; their new positioning meant that they would actually now be trapped between that army and the walls of Damascus.

ONCE OUT OF THE SHADE OF THE ORCHARDS, THE CRUSADERS AND THEIR HORSES SIMPLY BAKED UNCOMFORTABLY IN THE SUN.

Morale among the crusaders plunged, and after depressed strategic deliberations, it was decided that the only option was to withdraw. Here was essentially the end of the Second Crusade. The retreat began on 29 July, and was harried all the way by the now ebullient Muslim forces of Damascus. Among the Franks, there were dark mutterings about treason and betrayal. Some even argued that the decision to shift to the east of the city was planted by enemy agents and sympathizers. Over subsequent weeks, as both Louis and Conrad and most of their surviving soldiers retreated ignominiously back through Anatolia and on to Western Europe, these rumours of betrayal broadened in scope. Louis in particular started to deflect responsibility by blaming the Byzantines for collaborating with the enemy, citing their treaty with Nur al-Din. Bernard of Clairvaux obligingly gave this interpretation a theological gloss, explaining God's displeasure with Byzantine collaboration as a reason for the collapse of the Second Crusade. There were even those who advocated a subsequent crusade against Constantinople itself. Conrad, meanwhile, put blame and suspicion largely upon Baldwin III, for his role in the decision to shift forces to the east of the city. Some also pointed to fractures in the crusader leadership, particularly the acrimony generated by promises from the western leadership that Count Thierry of Flanders might be given Damascus after its liberation, a pledge that alienated many others in Outremer and Constantinople.

Surveying the Second Crusade, we see a multitude of influences, personalities and decisions behind the outcomes. What was certain, however, was that the Second Crusade ended

Below: An idealized fifteenth-century vision of the crusaders besieging Damascus in 1148. The decision to move away from the main water supplies was a key reason for the failure of the siege.

with Outremer strategically weakened, the Christian rulers split by dissent and, more important, the Muslim world united in a way it had not been for many decades, scenting further blood.

NUR AL-DIN AND THE CONTROL OF SYRIA

By April 1149, both Conrad and Louis were back in Western Europe. For the Crusader States a four-decade struggle was just beginning, one that would lead in 1187 to the unthinkable (for the Christians) – the recapture of Jerusalem by the Muslims.

Back in 1149, however, that event seemed a distant and unreal prospect. Yet there was no doubt that the Outremer was on the back foot, suddenly under more intense potential threat from a galvanized Islamic world. It was around this time that the language of *jihad*, particularly in relation to the 'lesser' *jihad* against non-Muslim enemies (as against the 'greater' *jihad* with oneself), became more prominent, if only as a rhetorical device. Certainly, by the end of the 1140s and early 1150s, the Crusader States seemed on the back foot. Nur al-Din made incursions into Outremer east of the Orontes River, in his efforts to take two crusader outposts, at Apamea and Harim.

YET THERE WAS NO DOUBT THAT THE OUTREMER WAS ON THE BACK FOOT, SUDDENLY UNDER MORE INTENSE POTENTIAL THREAT FROM A GALVANIZED ISLAMIC WORLD.

At the resulting battle of Inab on 29 June 1149, Nur al-Din wiped out an army led by Raymond of Antioch in a five-hour battle. One of the crusader dead was Raymond himself; his decapitated head, ornamented in silver, was sent as a token of victory to the caliph of Baghdad. Raymond's death left Antioch with a succession crisis, and it was only resolved when Baldwin III, King of Jerusalem (r. 1143–63) – son of Melisende and Fulk – stepped into the position as ruler of both kingdoms. Furthermore, in 1152 Raymond II of Tripoli was murdered by Muslim Assassins, and Baldwin had to take rule of Tripoli as well. Bearing in mind that he was only 19 at this time, the administrative and psychological burden must have been formidable, especially as he was facing such a wily and formidable operator as Nur al-Din.

THE ASSASSINS

THE ASSASSINS WERE A clandestine Muslim sect formed under the Fatimid caliphate by Hassan-i-Sabbah, leader of the Nizari Ismailites, a branch of Shia Islam emerging from the late eleventh century. From a remote mountain base in northern Syria, Hassan-i-Sabbah oversaw the recruitment and training of young men to serve as *fidayeen*, killers who would conduct missions to assassinate prominent figures in the Sunni military and political leadership. The new recruits, often first drugged with hashish, were indoctrinated in beautiful surroundings, replete with food and available women, and made to feel that they were fulfilling a sacred duty. What emerged were competent killers. One of their most prominent victims was the Seljuk vizier Nizam al-Mulk, but their killing of Raymond II of Tripoli showed that they did not just limit their focus to the Muslim world.

Left: Hassan-i-Sabbah oversees the initiation of a new recruit into the ranks of the assassins. Hassan was known as the 'Old Man of the Mountain'.

Baldwin III

Despite his youth, Baldwin proved to be a confident ruler. In 1153, he took an army south and, after a siege lasting from January to August, reclaimed the important Fatimid frontier city of Ascalon. He also oversaw some important political manoeuvres that strengthened his kingdoms. He facilitated a marriage between Raymond's widow, Constance of Hauteville, and the knight Raynald of Châtillon, thereby bringing some measure of stability to Antioch, although Raynald's brutal and hot-headed attitude would later attract much strife to Outremer. He also

rebuilt relations with Byzantium, principally through marriage alliances: he married Theodora Comnena, the niece of Manuel I, in September 1158, and in return Manuel married Maria of Antioch, the daughter of Constance and the late Raymond. The combination of military victories (including the recapture of Harim in 1158) and strategic alliances meant that Outremer's security seemed preserved.

Another element in Outremer's favour was that Nur al-Din's attention was largely directed elsewhere. During the 1150s–1170s, his principal objectives were to consolidate Syria under his single rule and also to overthrow the heretical Fatimid dynasty. He practically accomplished the first objective through his occupation of Damascus in April 1154. Ironically, given the rising spirit of *jihad* in his domain and the openly expressed desire to return the Holy Land to Islamic control, he also agreed a series of truces with Baldwin in the early 1160s, largely freeing him to pursue his Egyptian ambitions – these were days of the most spontaneous and erratic pragmatism. In 1163, Nur al-Din had signed a truce with the Byzantine Empire as well.

NUR AL-DIN'S ... PRINCIPAL OBJECTIVES WERE TO CONSOLIDATE SYRIA UNDER HIS SINGLE RULE AND ALSO TO OVERTHROW THE HERETICAL FATIMID DYNASTY.

The Crusader States were also militarily aggressive towards the Fatimids. Indeed, Baldwin III died on 10 February 1163 and was succeeded by Amalric, younger son of Melisende and Fulk. One of his earliest military actions was an unsuccessful invasion of Egypt in September 1163, the first of five such invasions conducted in the remainder of the 1160s. It was clear that the Fatimids were being pressured by both the Turks and the Crusader States, although this would not prevent the latter signing opportunistic truces later in the period, as the Turkish threat intensified.

With the death of Baldwin, relations between Nur al-Din and Outremer took another downturn. As Amalric was distracted with his Egyptian invasion, Nur al-Din took the opportunity to invade Tripoli. The subsequent campaign was far harder than Nur al-Din might have predicted. His armies

Opposite: The crusader king Baldwin III of Jerusalem is here shown in saintly detail in a stained glass window in the Basilica of the Holy Blood, Bruges, Belgium.

suffered a significant defeat at the battle of al-Buqaia in 1163, but the setback was spectacularly reversed on 12 August 1164 at the battle of Harim (Harenc). He utilized the classic Seljuk manoeuvre of feigned retreat to draw a huge crusader army – it included forces from the County of Tripoli, the Principality of Antioch, the Byzantine Empire and Armenia – into a trap, where it was destroyed, with most of the crusader leaders becoming Nur al-Din's prisoners, later to be ransomed. Nur al-Din now had Antioch itself in his grasp, but judiciously chose not to take the city and risk further open warfare with Byzantium. Thus, with his Syrian territories secure, he refocused his efforts on Egypt once more.

Above: The battle of Harim (Harenc) on 12 August 1164 was a disaster for the crusader armies, their casualties possibly being as high as 10,000 men.

THE RISE OF SALADIN

In April 1164, Nur al-Din launched an invasion of Egyptian territory. As he was at this time occupied with fighting the Franks, the Egyptian operation was led by the corpulent Kurdish general Asad al-Din Shirkuh, aided by his nephew, Salah al-Din Yusuf, as his second-in-command. Western history came to know Salah al-Din Yusuf as Saladin, arguably the greatest of the Muslim commanders and rulers during this period.

In January 1169, Shirkuh's Syrian army again pushed hard into Egypt, following closely on the heels of another Frankish invasion of Egypt. Alexandria was taken, then held by Saladin, as Shirkuh pushed on to Cairo, entering the city now under the invitation of the Fatimids themselves – they wanted Nur al-Din's assistance in repelling the Franks. Shirkuh stayed on, being appointed vizier – essentially the Fatimid first minister. Then in March 1169, Shirkuh died of a heart attack and into his shoes

SALADIN

Left: A lively sixteenth-century portrait of the great Saladin, the founder of the Ayyubid dynasty and scourge of the Crusader States.

BORN IN 1137/38 in Tikrit, Saladin hailed from an influential Kurdish family. As a young man, Saladin showed a preoccupation with religious studies, and throughout his life he would always have a strong academic side to his personality, making him an urbane and informed ruler, with sophistication in diplomacy. He also demonstrated talent as a military commander, and it was this fusion of military and political skills that eventually led to his being the unchallenged commander of the Muslim world in the late twelfth century. He was dedicated to the pursuit of *jihad*, but at the same time he was pragmatic and, when the time was right, merciful. Having said this, Saladin was more than capable of summoning the brutality of the age. After the Frankish defeat at Hattin in 1187, for example, Saladin dispatched the surviving low-rank Templars and Hospitallers by having the untrained Muslim civilians and scholars in his army amateurishly hack the men to death, while he looked on from a podium. But such actions were more aberrations than norms, and even in the west Saladin was known as a civilized figure.

stepped Saladin as vizier, who proceeded to spread the cultural and political influence of both his own family and Sunni Islam through Egypt, weakening Fatimid control. Saladin was now, in effect, also in control of Egypt's military, and with his enhanced capability he quashed Amalric's final Egyptian invasion, breaking the combined Byzantine/Frankish siege of Damietta in December.

Two further mortal events pushed Saladin's authority even higher. The first was the death of the Fatimid caliph, al-Adid, on 13 September 1171 (there were rumours that he had been

Above: This dual artwork depicts the death of Amalric I of Jerusalem on the left, and the subsequent coronation of Amalric's son, Baldwin IV, at the age of just 13.

poisoned). Instead of replacing him in Cairo, Saladin changed all references in state prayers to the Sunni caliph in Baghdad, thereby heralding the advent of the Ayyubid dynasty, named after Saladin's father, Ayub. The second was the death of Nur al-Din on 15 May 1174. Tensions between Saladin and Nur al-Din had been growing for years, Nur al-Din rightly suspecting that Saladin was building an independent fiefdom. With Nur al-Din's death, factions vied for power in Syria and Mesopotamia, but ultimately Saladin's combination of smart, patient statecraft and military threat proved unstoppable. He took over Damascus in 1174, then steadily brought more and more pieces of the Muslim world under his control. Aleppo, the most resistant of the cities, finally relented to him in 1183.

For Outremer, these were critically dangerous times – Muslim unity raised the prospect of a mass, coordinated *jihad* against the Crusader States, which were now wrapped in Muslim territory. Furthermore, Outremer's government was in a state of flux once more. Amalric died on 11 July 1174, his successor being King Baldwin IV of Jerusalem, just 13 years old on his ascent to the troubled throne. He had the additional burden of suffering from leprosy, hence his ever-sensitive nickname, 'The Leper King'. Sensing that Baldwin was not destined for a long life, various factions within the court jostled for power and influence, scattering the focus that was really required to counter Saladin's threat.

A Broken Truce

This being said, Outremer was still replete with competent warriors and veterans. Saladin was reminded of this fact in November 1177, when his army was defeated by a relatively small force of crusader knights, who attacked and scattered a Muslim army near Montisgard as Saladin advanced on Jerusalem. There were other battles, with victories and defeats on both sides, leading Baldwin and Saladin to make a two-year truce in 1180.

Two years proved too much for some. The aforementioned Raynald of Châtillon, by now the lord of the great castle of al-Karak in Oultrejordain (he had remarried wisely following the death of his first wife), was bullishly hostile to any notion of rapprochement with the Muslims, and attacked Muslim pilgrims

Below: In this painting of the battle of Montgisard (25 November 1177), the physically afflicted 16-year-old Baldwin IV is carried into combat on the shoulders of his men.

on the routes to Mecca and raided trade caravans. The truce therefore dissolved, and Saladin made attacks into the Kingdom of Jerusalem and Oultrejordain in late 1183, although both were repulsed.

IT WAS AT THIS POINT, HOWEVER, THAT SALADIN – EMERGING FROM A LONG PERIOD OF ILLNESS – BEGAN PREPARATIONS FOR HIS FINAL EFFORT TO QUASH THE POWER OF THE CRUSADER STATES.

In May 1185, King Baldwin IV died aged 23. Despite his tragic illness, he had surprised all with his astonishing bravery and self-control. Towards the end of his reign, he would even ride out with his knights, tied physically onto his horse to prevent his falling off. He was replaced with another youth, this time the even younger Baldwin V, just six years old and also seriously ill. His regent, Raymond III of Tripoli, was transparently angling for power, a fact that brought him into conflict with other interested parties. Such was the tension that the Patriarch of Jerusalem, Heraclius, and the masters of the Templars and Hospitallers, even travelled to Britain to request that King Henry II take up the kingship of Jerusalem, an optimistic hope that was turned down after due consideration. Philip II of France was also asked, and similarly declined.

Baldwin V lasted only a year as king before his untimely death in September 1186. There immediately began a sordid power grab, in which Raymond III was beaten to the throne by Sybylla (Baldwin IV's sister) and her husband Guy of Lusignan. It was at this point, however, that Saladin – emerging from a long period of illness – began preparations for his final effort to quash the power of the Crusader States.

Above: Guy de Lusignan, King of Jerusalem, presided over the ignominious fall of Jerusalem to the Muslims in October 1187, an event that led to the triggering of the Third Crusade.

SALADIN'S TRIUMPH – THE BATTLE OF HATTIN

Moved to action by the aggressive behaviour of Raynald, plus the expiration of another truce with the Franks, Saladin began making incursions into Outremer in the spring of 1187, building up to his ultimate objective – the capture of Jerusalem. In an indication of Raymond III's disaffection, he even permitted some 7000 Muslim cavalry to pass through his lands unhindered on a reconnaissance mission. Actually, some 150 Templars, unaware of the accommodation, made a suicidal attack against the Muslims at Cresson near Nazareth, and were killed almost to a man.

Raymond now saw the scale of the Muslim thunderclouds gathering on the horizon, and allied himself with King Guy of Jerusalem. Together, the Crusader States drew up an army of about 16,000 warriors, certainly a sizeable force, but one still dwarfed by the c. 30,000 men-at-arms that Saladin now led across the River Jordan, just south of the Sea of Galilee.

What followed now has become one of those object lessons in tactical failure that are taught in military colleges around the world. The Franks made their camp at al-Saffuriyah, a well-watered and defendable position about 10km (6 miles) north of Nazareth. Saladin needed to lure them out into the open if he was to crush them, and thus he besieged the city of Tiberias on the coast of the Sea of Galilee. It so happened that Raymond's wife, Countess Eschiva, governed the city, which fell quickly, with Eschiva and other nobles taking refuge in the citadel.

Amongst the Frankish army, there was now a heated debate about the course of action. Raymond, actually showing great restraint, argued against attempting the relief of Tiberias, stating that such was Saladin's intention and that the long, arid road to the city would cause logistical and health problems on the march. King Guy sided with him, as did many others. Yet some – principally Gerard of Ridfort and the firebrand Raynald – argued otherwise, and even planted the idea that Raymond was actually a traitor and that the only action of merit was to eject the infidels

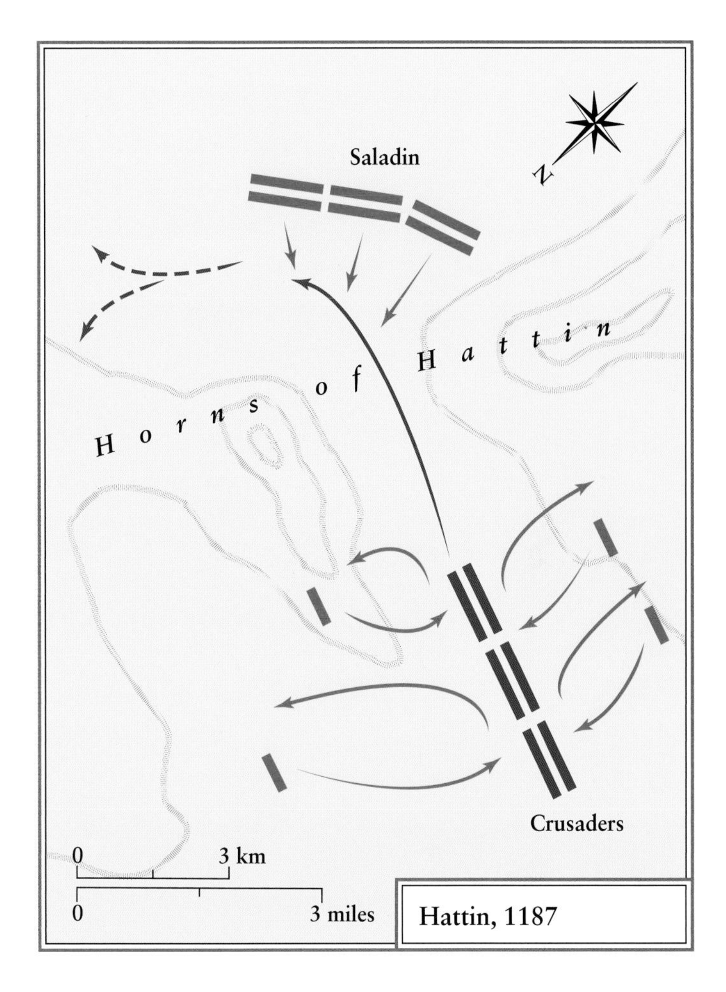

Above: A map of the battle of Hattin, showing how Saladin used the geological features around him to channel, trap and destroy the crusader army.

from the Holy Land. Steadily their arguments gained traction, and on 3 July, as the sun ominously crested the horizon, the crusader army left al-Saffuriyah and headed east. Saladin, forewarned, was delighted – the crusaders were walking into his trap.

Tiberias was theoretically about a day's march from al-Saffuriyah, but within just a few hours the men, clad in steel and cloth armour, began to suffer greatly from heat exhaustion and dehydration. Saladin had sealed up the wells on the route of travel, hence water supplies quickly ran out. The thick clouds of throat-drying dust only added to the dreadful nature of the experience. As the Franks advanced, the Muslim cavalry now began to harry the rearguard incessantly, stretching out the crusader column and weakening its integrity, plus inflicting casualties. This went on all day, and finally the army had to make camp for the night, still about 10km (6 miles) from Tiberias, approaching a rocky two-pronged geological feature known as the Horns of Hattin, the remnants of an extinct volcano. The crusaders set out again at first light, but Saladin bided his time,

Below: Crusader knights, many of them dismounted (large numbers of horses had died from dehydration), are overwhelmed by a charge from Saladin's cavalry.

waiting until midday – by which time the sun would be at its most extreme – before launching a massive archery attack. To add to the Franks' confusion and misery, the Muslims set fire to the surrounding grass, creating dense clouds of smoke and embers that stung eyes and dried out already parched throats. King Guy drew his surviving forces up around the Horns of Hattin, where his knights fought with astonishing bravery. But the outcome was inevitable, and finally those who hadn't been killed were brought into captivity. Most of the nobles were treated with respect by Saladin, King Guy given a drink of cool water; the exception was Raynald, whom Saladin struck with a sword, before a guard completed the job by severing Raynald's head.

MOST OF THE NOBLES WERE TREATED WITH RESPECT BY SALADIN, KING GUY GIVEN A DRINK OF COOL WATER; THE EXCEPTION WAS RAYNALD, WHOM SALADIN STRUCK WITH A SWORD.

THE FALL OF JERUSALEM

The dominoes began to fall quickly in Palestine. The citadel in Tiberias quickly capitulated, and Acre, Jaffa, Caesarea and Ascalon followed shortly after. But now came the ultimate prize for Saladin – Jerusalem. The great city was ill-prepared for a siege, as its new commander, Balian of Ibelin, discovered when he took over the defence. He had only about 60 skilled knights at his disposal, plus several thousand other men, although of highly variable quality. Panic was in the air, as recent history told the population that they could expect little mercy if they resisted and were then defeated.

Saladin arrived at the city on 20 September, and there followed six days of intensive fighting, the Muslims unable to push inside the walls despite the thunderous pounding of siege engines and the efforts of undermining (a breach was made on 29 September, but it was successfully defended). Then, at the end of September, Balian approached Saladin with a proposition for peaceful surrender, loaded with the threat that if Saladin didn't accept, the 5000 Muslims still within Jerusalem would be slaughtered, plus the Muslim holy places destroyed. Saladin

Above: The surrender of the crusaders to Saladin after Hattin. King Guy, shown mercy, sits next to Saladin while Reynald – soon to be executed – lays down his sword.

agreed to the surrender, but only on condition that a monetary ransom was paid for each of the Christians, to secure their safety through purchase. The anonymous *De Expugnatione Terrae Sanctae per Saladinum* (*The Capture of the Holy Land by Saladin*), written shortly after the war, possibly by a Templar or Hospitaller, recounts both the conditions of the ransom and the despair of the ultimate surrender:

> *Saladin had taken counsel and laid down these ransom terms for the inhabitants of Jerusalem: each male, ten years old and over, was to pay ten besants for his ransom; females,*

> *five besants; boys, seven years old and under, one. Those who wished would be freed on these terms and could leave securely with their possessions. The inhabitants of Jerusalem who would not accept these terms, or those who did not have ten besants, were to become booty, to be slain by the army's swords. This agreement pleased the lord Patriarch and the others who had money...*
>
> *But, alas, by the hands of wicked Christians Jerusalem was turned over to the wicked. The gates were closed and guards were posted. The* fakihs *and* kadis *[judges], the ministers of the wicked error, who are considered bishops and priests by the Saracens came for prayer and religious purposes first to the Temple of the Lord, which they call Beithhalla and in which they have great faith for salvation. They believed they were cleansing it and with unclean and horrible bellows they defiled the Temple by shouting with polluted lips the Muslim precept:* 'Allahu akbar! Allahu akbar! . . .' *[God is Great]*
> *Our people held the city of Jerusalem for some eighty-nine years... Within a short time, Saladin had conquered almost the whole Kingdom of Jerusalem. He exalted the grandeur of Muhammad's law and showed that, in the event, its might exceeded that of the Christian religion.*

The fall of Jerusalem was, in a sense, an extension of the disastrous Second Crusade. Its downfall reflected a Frankish society riven with factions, which contrasted with the rise of an increasingly unified and purposeful Muslim world under Saladin. For a time, both Byzantium and Western Europe had lost interest in Outremer, disaffected by its dramas and reluctant to get sucked into any more money-hungry campaigns. With the fall of Jerusalem, the greatest city in Christendom, however, the wider world was now paying attention.

THE FALL OF JERUSALEM ... REFLECTED A FRANKISH SOCIETY RIVEN WITH FACTIONS, WHICH CONTRASTED WITH THE RISE OF AN INCREASINGLY UNIFIED AND PURPOSEFUL MUSLIM WORLD UNDER SALADIN.

4

Two Kings Journey to the Holy Land

The Third Crusade (1187–92) was meant to rectify the disasters of the Second, and restore Christian supremacy in the Holy Land. This time, the direct involvement of three monarchs – Richard I of England, Philip II of France and the German Emperor Frederick I – brought together a coalition of seemingly unrivalled power. Yet by the end of the Crusade, against all expectations, Jerusalem remained in the hands of Saladin.

The fall of Jerusalem convulsed the Christian world. That the Holy City, until recently nestled securely amongst the Crusader States – now themselves significantly contracted – could pass back under the control of Islam had been unthinkable. Such was the impact of the news upon the elderly and sick Pope Urban III that it was said he died of shock, passing away on 20 October 1187. There must have been something in the air, for the new Pope, Gregory VIII, held the papacy for a mere 57 days, before succumbing to

Opposite: King Philip II of France watches over the surrender of the population of Acre, which fell in July 1191 after a six-week siege imposed by Philip and Richard I.

Above: Pope Gregory VIII issued the call for the Third Crusade following reports of the capture of Jerusalem and the horrific crusader defeat at Hattin.

a fever and dying on 17 December 1187. During his brief spell as leader of the Catholic Christian Church, however, Gregory issued the bull *Audita Tremendi*. This document, replete with emotion, penitence and resistance, made it clear that blame for the catastrophe in the Middle East was, to a large degree, laid at the feet of the Christian world, which had displayed its divided and sinful nature.

On this basis, Gregory called for a further Crusade, again tempting the great and the good with the promise of a plenary indulgence. This new Crusade would in many ways be the ultimate act of repentance.

ROYAL ARMIES

The *Audita Tremendi* was issued in October 1187, but the wheels of mobilization, politics and statecraft turned slowly – armies would not begin the campaign march until May 1189. Between those two dates, the great and the good of Western Europe responded with an unprecedented level of royal involvement. Indeed, unlike the First Crusade, which had no monarch at its head, the Third Crusade would have no fewer than three: King Philip II of France, King Richard I of England, and Frederick Barbarossa, Emperor of Germany.

Philip II (r. 1180–1223) was a young king, just 15 years of age when he took the throne, and only 22 at the time he took the cross, alongside Henry II, in January 1188. The common focus offered by the Crusade (both had been inspired to join following a spellbinding sermon on the topic by Archbishop Joscius of Tyre) temporarily papered over the cracks between the two monarchs, although fighting between the French and English thrones would recommence within months.

GREGORY CALLED FOR A FURTHER CRUSADE, AGAIN TEMPTING THE GREAT AND THE GOOD WITH THE PROMISE OF A PLENARY INDULGENCE.

Richard I (r. 1189–99), son of Henry II and Eleanor of Aquitaine, was the Count of Poitou and the Duke of Aquitaine at the point he took the cross in November 1187. Henry II also took the cross, in January 1188, but any martial intentions were undone by his death on 6 July 1189 while on campaign in France, at the age of just 56. (He had actually been fighting a rebellious Richard, his own son, over inheritance and land rights in France.) Thus, Richard took the throne.

Richard I would be the archetypal warrior king. His epithet 'Richard the Lionheart' was fully justified – he was brave and skilled in battle, ruthlessly disciplined in handling his armies, a talented strategist and tactician. He also wielded that distinctly medieval mix of excessive brutality and canny diplomacy. Crucially, however, he had an eye for administration and finance, principles that would underpin his ability both to deliver a Crusade and to rule over the extensive Angevin Empire. To fund his eastern campaign, and particularly an extensive shipbuilding programme (he opted for maritime deployment to Outremer, rather than the slower and more risky overland route), Richard

Below: The coronation of Philip Augustus as Philip II at the cathedral of Reims, 1 November 1179. He was only 14 at this time, but grew to be a highly competent ruler, building the power of the French state in Europe.

relied upon the imposition of an unpopular war tax first levied by Henry. Appropriately enough, the tax was known as the 'Saladin tithe'.

Richard's motivation for participating in the Crusade is unclear, but genuine religious enthusiasm does seem to be a working factor. The drive must have been strong, for in many ways Richard's interests would have been better served by staying at home. Rivalries between the English and French kings over Angevin territories led to periodic conflicts, and Richard's relationship with Philip II was turbulent and variable. The fact that Philip himself took the cross at the same time as Richard was ultimately insurance for both men, and indeed a precondition for their participation; if they were deployed at the same time, they knew that there was less chance of trouble back home. Furthermore, although Richard was technically a feudal vassal of Philip, on account of the Angevin lands in France (Normandy, Anjou and Aquitaine), Richard actually had deeper financial pockets and a larger and more potent army. For a time at least, the two men's interests would balance each other out.

The greatest of the royal participants in the Third Crusade was Frederick I (r. 1155–90), known by the epithet 'Barbarossa', meaning 'Red Beard'. It was Frederick who introduced, in 1157, the term 'Holy Empire' to define his lands, just two years after he took the throne in 1155. Frederick was the oldest of the crusading monarchs by a good measure – he was in his mid-60s at the point he took the cross in March 1188. Yet he remained a powerful and heroic figure, one who garnered loyalty and inspired thousands of others to commit themselves to the German element of the Crusade. It is said that at the celebration of Pentecost in Mainz, Germany, in 1188, some 13,000 men took the cross, inspired partly through the inspired preaching of Bishop Godfrey of Würzburg and partly through the excited commitment of Frederick himself.

Opposite: King Richard I, aka Richard the Lionheart. Richard was a sage, hard-driving ruler, intolerant of indiscipline amongst his men, although he was also known for being sexually promiscuous and financially greedy.

Below: A statue of Frederick I 'Barbarossa'. Had he not died from an accident, the outcome of the Third Crusade could well have been very different.

JEWISH MASSACRES IN ENGLAND, 1189–90

Above: The massacre of Jews during the coronation of King Richard I at Westminster Abbey on 3 September 1189.

In both the First and the Second Crusades anti-Jewish pogroms were a dark counterpoint to the crusading spirit. Upon Richard I's coronation on 3 September 1189, such impulses were again unleashed, this time within England. During his coronation alone, emotions ran high when a mob witnessed high-ranking Jewish citizens paying homage to the king in Westminster Abbey. They rioted, killing dozens in London's Jewish quarter. Richard immediately attempted to clamp down on the violence, but the anti-Semitic campaign spread progressively through England through late 1189 and in the first three months of 1190.

Particularly vicious attacks were recorded at King's Lynn, Colchester, Thetford, Ospringe, Stamford, Lincoln and Bury St Edmunds – 57 Jews were massacred in the latter alone. The worst of the instances, however, occurred in York, where anti-Jewish riots forced dozens of Jews to take refuge in the city's castle. Recognizing that unless they converted to Christianity they would be massacred, a large number of Jews hiding in a castle tower chose to commit suicide; the men killed their wives and children first, then set the tower on fire so that their bodies might not be desecrated. All those who surrendered to the mob outside were killed. On these fateful days in mid-March, 150 Jews were massacred, and York's centuries-old Jewish community was no more.

Frederick brought much to the Third Crusade. In addition to wealth and a large army, Frederick contributed experience – he had fought in the Second Crusade (his uncle was Conrad III). For the papacy, his participation also brought a cessation to the prolonged conflict between the Church and the German Empire. Saladin's victories in the east had, by consequence, brought together a triumvirate of immense power. The total strength of the armies of the Third Crusade may have numbered in excess of 100,000.

Above: Frederick I 'Barbarossa' led one of the greatest Crusader forces ever gathered. He was famous for his organizational skills and battlefield acumen, as well as for his red beard.

THE GERMAN CAMPAIGN

From January 1188, Saladin received increasing reports of the scale of the Crusade building against him in Europe. From the high point of his capture of Jerusalem, his power had weakened somewhat, challenged both by internal squabbles within the Muslim kingdoms and also by some plucky continuing resistance from within the Crusader States, which were now anchored particularly on Antioch, Tripoli and Tyre.

At first, it appeared as if the defeated Crusader States might be more intent upon fighting amongst themselves rather than facing Saladin. In April 1189, Guy of Lusignan, King of Jerusalem, laid siege to Tyre, the domain of Conrad of Montferrat, who had only recently fought off a siege by Saladin's forces in the winter of 1187–88. Yet following his reinforcement by forces from Pisa, Guy marched south with 600 knights and 7000 infantry and besieged Muslim-held Acre instead.

The siege was a tactically curious one, the dispositions of the rival troops gaining greater significance with the later arrival of the crusaders. Guy placed his siege lines about a mile inland from Acre, anchored in the foothills of Mount Turon. Saladin, showing an unusual caution, moved up a large relief army but did not throw it into a major attack, stretching it out instead about 8km (5 miles) to the east of Guy's positions. Thus, a curious and at times almost convivial stalemate ensued, with Acre, resilient enough to keep the enemy at bay, under siege from the Franks, and the Franks virtually under siege from Saladin.

AS SALADIN STRUGGLED WITH THE SIEGE OF ACRE, THE CRUSADING ARMIES FROM EUROPE WERE ON THEIR WAY.

The nearby ocean altered the dynamics of this equation, however, as Guy received substantial reinforcements via amphibious landings, including a large force of northern Europeans in August 1189.

As Saladin struggled with the siege of Acre, the crusading armies from Europe were on their way. The Third Crusade is roughly broken down into two separate strands: the campaign by Frederick's German forces, and the later joint (temporarily at least) Anglo-French effort.

FREDERICK'S CRUSADE

Frederick's crusade began in May 1188, his army evincing scale and professionalism. Indeed, both Frederick and Richard were notable for the strict bonds of discipline that they imposed over their armies, weeding out many unsuitable elements, such as valueless camp followers and criminal types, and imposing often mortal punishments on those who broke the rules, particularly in relation to unwarranted violent or abusive behaviour. The Germans set off from Ratisbon (Regensburg) on the long overland route towards the Byzantine Empire and Anatolia. As always, the Byzantine Emperor – since 1185 Isaac II Angelos – watched the approaching crusaders with some trepidation. Relations between Constantinople and the German Empire had always been brittle, and in the Byzantine Balkans there was some minor fighting that even escalated into Frederick's seeking approval from the Pope for the Crusade to be redirected against the Byzantine Empire. Thankfully for the Crusade, this plan did not come to fruition (the Fourth Crusade, as we shall see, was another matter). Isaac, keen to steer the Germans away from

Constantinople itself, shipped the crusader army across the Dardanelles into Anatolia.

In time-honoured fashion, the Germans suffered from the same maladies as all crusader armies previously crossing Anatolia – hunger, thirst, weariness and the regular harassing attacks from Seljuk Turkish tribes, despite the fact that in the recent past Frederick had even attempted to form a German–Seljuk pact with the Sultanate of Rum. Nevertheless, despite the adversity, Frederick's troops had sufficient force to capture the Seljuk capital, Iconium, on 17 May. This victory unsettled Saladin, and he then watched the Germans advance onwards to the borders of Armenia.

But capricious fate would step in on Saladin's side. On 10 June 1190, Frederick drowned in relatively shallow waters of the River Saleph, in Cicilian Armenia. The exact cause of the drowning remains something of a mystery, although the likeliest explanation is simply a heart attack, brought on by a tired, older man venturing into cold water. With the noble centre now ripped out of the army, which already had a 50 per cent reduced strength, many of the German soldiers decided against continuing and turned for home. A small number of the more committed,

Below: An artwork in a medieval illuminated manuscript depicts Frederick I on crusade, his banners displaying the black eagle of the Holy Roman Empire.

Opposite: As depicted rather fancifully in this manuscript artwork, Richard I Lionheart invaded and captured the island of Cyprus in 1191, during his transit to the Levant.

led by Frederick of Swabia, stayed with the Crusade, marching onwards until they reached the siege of Acre in October 1190.

TWO KINGS JOURNEY TO THE HOLY LAND

The French and British journey to the Holy Land began on 4 July 1190, both of the armies setting out together from Vézelay in northern Burgundy. They travelled south on foot until they reached Lyon, then parted ways, Richard heading for Marseilles and Philip for Genoa, from where both would pick up maritime transport to Outremer. Philip's ships would take the most direct route, sailing straight through the Straits of Messina before heading directly across the Mediterranean to Acre. Richard, meanwhile, would sail in a series of short hops down the western Italian coastline, through the Straits of Messina, across to Crete and then Cyprus, before the final crossing to Acre.

Richard's journey was by far the more eventful of the two. The Sicilian king, Tancred of Lecce, had taken Queen Joanna – the wife of the former king and also, as it happened, Richard's sister – prisoner in Messina. Having reached Sicily in September 1190, Richard demanded her release, which was grudgingly implemented, but tensions between the crusaders and the Sicilians remained high, leading to some combat and Richard's de facto occupation of Messina. Richard spent several more months on Sicily, even fitting in a marriage to Berengaria, the daughter of the King of Navarre.

Nor was Sicily the end of Richard's in-transit adventures. At Cyprus – Byzantine territory – some of the occupants of British ships, including Joanna and Berengaria, were taken prisoner by the Cypriot king, Isaac Comnenus, after their boats were blown ashore in rough

Below: Richard I strides triumphantly atop the fortifications at Messina, having attacked the city even while Philip II was lodged there.

estoit a mechinee Il y ala et y passa
son yuer auec le roy Jusq̃s au mars

weather. Richard, incensed by this outrage, attacked and took the southern coastal city of Limassol, forcing Isaac to make a truce and to contribute financially to the Crusade. Yet Isaac backed out of the agreement quickly, and in response Richard then conquered the entire island in just four weeks, subsequently imposing a Roman Catholic regime on what had previously been Byzantine territory. From such seeds, centuries of future tension would grow. He left Cyprus with his army on 5 June, landing first at Tyre then at Acre on 8 June. Philip II was already there when Richard arrived, having arrived at the siege lines on 20 May, following a largely unproblematic trip, apart from some moments when both he and Richard were present on Sicily during the tensions there.

SIEGE OF ACRE

On arrival at Acre, both Richard and Philip were debilitated for several weeks owing to a tropical illness, or possibly scurvy. Nevertheless, the siege quickly went up a gear. Crusaders built and brought up a large number of powerful siege engines, pummelling the city walls with boulders and arrows, digging beneath the foundations in undermining operations, while making assaults against the outer defences with siege towers and scaling ladders. The defenders of the city fought back with determination, showering those outside with a variety of missiles, including the terrifying Greek fire, an adhesive, burning substance projected over several metres by bellows.

After weeks of punishment, and with the city walls starting to crumble, Acre's resolve began to soften.

After weeks of punishment, and with the city walls starting to crumble, Acre's resolve began to soften. The Franks had also built their own defensive walls between themselves and Saladin, which kept the potential relief army at bay. On 4 July a messenger from the city began to talk about the possibilities of a truce, and on 12 July this became a full-blown peace negotiation, with Conrad of Tyre at the helm for the crusaders. A surrender agreement was reached, based on the defenders paying a large ransom; an additional 3000 of the inhabitants were held as

SIEGE ENGINES

SIEGE ENGINES WERE MECHANISMS designed for the assault or penetration of fortresses. The principal siege engines of the medieval era, and the types used during the siege of Acre, were as follows:

BATTERING RAMS – Battering rams (below) ranged from small, pointed logs swung by hand by 4–6 men, through to massive wheeled systems swinging metal-capped tree trunks weighing several tonnes. Battering rams might also be mounted in the upper floors of siege towers.

BORERS – Borers were essentially torsion-powered drills, used to bore through weak points in masonry and timber.

CATAPULTS AND TORSION ENGINES – These were large, crew-operated weapons designed to throw boulders or heavy bolts to long ranges, using either sprung metal or rope torsion springs to fire the missile. Many of these weapons resembled over-sized, frame-mounted catapults.

TREBUCHETS – The heavy artillery of the ancient and medieval world, some trebuchets (see left) were capable of throwing stones weighing 100kg (220lb) to distances of more than 200m (650ft), demolishing walls and defences. A trebuchet missile at the siege of Acre was said to have killed 12 men in one missile strike. The long throwing arm of the trebuchet was powered either by traction (men pulling down on a rope attached to the short end) or by suddenly releasing a massive counterweight on the beam.

SIEGE TOWERS – These were wooden, multi-storey platforms mounted on wheels, allowing them to be pushed up the fortification walls for direct access via extending wooden walkways. The towers were often packed with missile weapons and archers to provide suppressive fire, while a covering of soaked hide panels protected against incendiary attacks.

hostages although later, on 20 August, Richard had 2700 of them beheaded outside the city, as trust between the two sides broke down – Saladin refused to relinquish the True Cross, which was in his possession, and prevaricated over the ransom payment. In this one ghastly act, the sight of which must have beggared belief, Richard demonstrated his ample capacity for brutality.

Above: Richard I could be a ruler without mercy. This scene shows, albeit in very Eurocentric fashion, the massacre of 2700 Muslim prisoners following the capture of Acre in 1191.

JAFFA AND ARSUF

Wanting to capitalize on the growing momentum that came from the capture of Acre, Richard now took his crusaders south, to wrest control of the stronghold of Jaffa, a distance of about 120km (75 miles) from Acre. After struggling to wrest the crusaders away from loot, wine and women, he finally got underway with about 15,000 men.

The march was going to be both exhausting and dangerous, travelling through summer heat and with the left flank of the army constantly exposed to raids and attacks from Saladin's warriors, now released from their positions around Acre. Famously, Richard formed his army into a well-regimented column. The baggage train presented the right wall of the column, protected by the sea and the crusader fleet to its immediate right. Richard was in the centre of the column, along with many of his nobles and a mixture of French and English soldiers. It should be noted that Philip was no longer with him; the French king had left the Crusade on 3 August to return to France, a decision that would later have significance as the Third Crusade played out. The elite Hospitallers formed the army's rearguard, while the van was led by the Templars. The left flank of the column was a large force of both infantry and archers, there to shield the king from the inevitable Muslim attacks.

Opposite: This artwork of a crusader assault upon Acre suggests something of the chaos of an attack against well-defended fortifications. The first warriors to ascend assault ladders were highly likely to die.

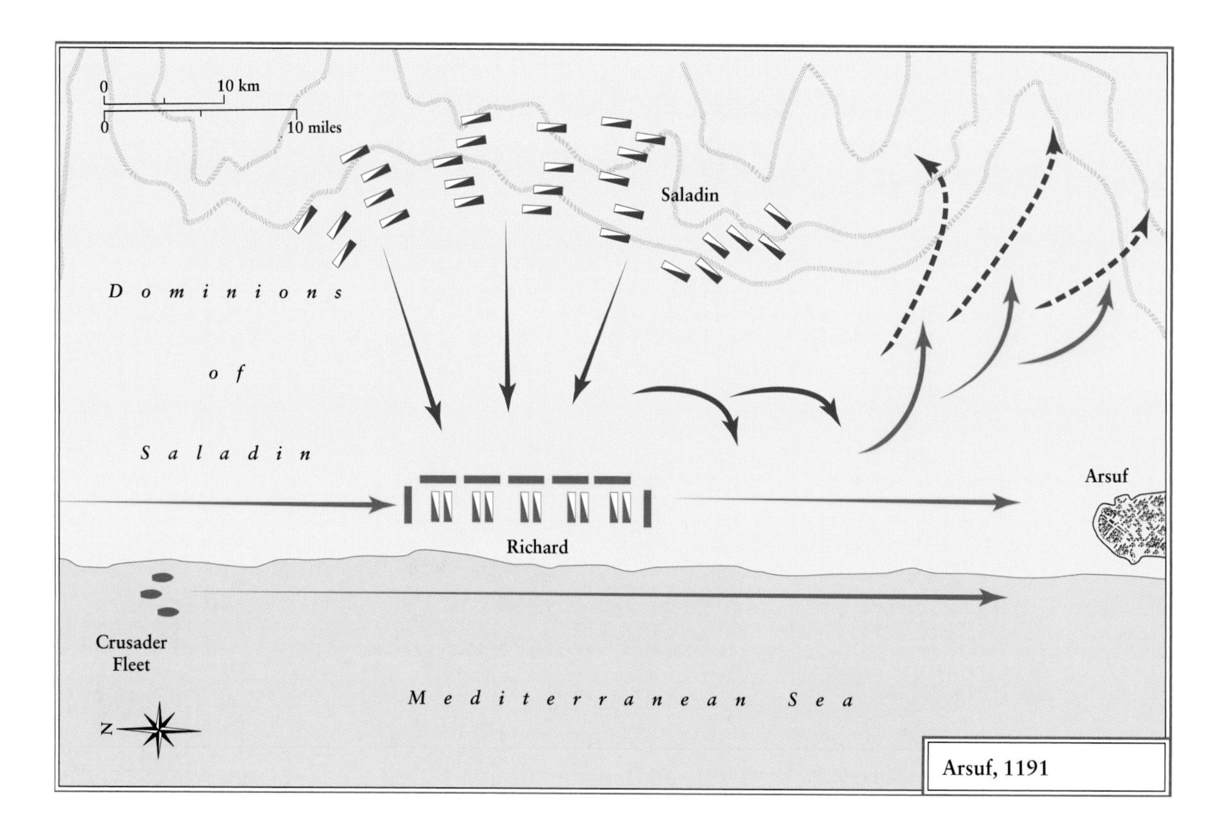

Above: The battle of Arsuf appeared to favour Saladin, who could attack a long, exposed flank, but a crusader victory was bought by a vigorous counter-charge.

The tightly-packed crusader column began its march. Richard knew that discipline was the absolute key to surviving the journey; his soldiers were under strict instructions not to pursue an enemy who was apparently retreating – the integrity of the information had to be preserved at all costs. In this way, Richard inched his army steadily down the coast, making about 8km (5 miles) of progress each day, while constantly under the arrows and the crossbow bolts of the enemy.

With exceptional fortitude, his men held the formation until, on 7 September, outside Arsuf (only 40km/25 miles from Jaffa), Saladin unleashed a mass offensive of 30,000 men, with himself in the frontlines urging his troops to victory. The desire of Christian troops to break ranks and charge became irresistible, and ultimately one that Richard could no longer restrain. His army charged en masse, and swept Saladin's forces from the field in a profound victory.

Richard lost around 700 men, while Saladin's casualties may have been as high as 7000. Aware of Richard's victory, the inhabitants of Jaffa now opened their gates and allowed the English king a bloodless takeover.

JERUSALEM – FROM SIEGE TO TREATY

For Richard, Jerusalem itself was the next logical step, the ultimate objective of the entire Crusade. Yet, from this point on, the inertia and complexity of war in the Holy Land, and further afield, began to exert their influence. Saladin, now fearing that the crusaders were building up to an offensive into Egypt, his powerbase, opted to destroy and abandon the southern city of Ascalon, on the coast opposite Jerusalem. By bringing the walls down, instead of defending them, Saladin was depriving Richard of an important staging base and port for an Egyptian offensive. Richard was also increasingly distracted by events back in Europe; there were rumours of Philip once again eyeing Richard's French territories.

Nevertheless, on 29 October 1191 Richard and his army moved out from Jaffa and advanced towards Jerusalem. The going, as ever, was extremely hard, made agonizing by a combination of winter weather and Saladin's attacks. During this phase, Richard involved himself in some adventurous diplomacy with Saladin's brother, al-Adil, actually going so far as to offer al-Adil his sister's hand in marriage, a considerate act of negotiation that, thankfully for Joanna, ultimately went nowhere. Aside from

Below: An idealized image of Richard I in action. His was still an age in which kings would participate directly in battle, and Richard was certainly a formidable warrior in his own right.

Richard's discussions, Conrad of Montferrat also discussed potential terms with Saladin, who suggested turning Acre over to the Sultan if he could be given the lordship of Sidon and Beirut. It was clear that many high-ranking crusaders were now looking for a way out of the campaign.

Richard's first march on Jerusalem came to nothing. At Beit Nuba, just 19km (12 miles) from the Holy City, he turned his exhausted army south-west to Ascalon, sensing that he did not have the manpower to take and hold Jerusalem. While his demoralized and also diminishing army (many were starting to leave the Crusade) set about rebuilding Ascalon, however, any Christian unity was breaking down, particularly in a dispute over who would become King of Jerusalem – Guy of Lusignan or Conrad of Montferrat. This dispute tipped over into fighting at Acre, and on 28 April 1192 Conrad was murdered, apparently by two Muslim assassins. Richard also received news, on 29 May, that back home his brother Prince John was making ambitious plottings with Philip. Clearly for Richard, it was time to finish up his business in the east, and head back west.

SALADIN, ENCOURAGED BY RICHARD'S SECOND PULLBACK FROM JERUSALEM, ATTACKED AND SEIZED THE CITY OF JAFFA.

First, Richard made another advance out to Jerusalem, again reaching Beit Nuba, on 10 June, before pushing across and taking up positions just outside the Holy City. From there, he launched a lightning attack against a major Egyptian supply caravan moving up to Jerusalem, ransacking the baggage train and acquiring large numbers of horses and camels. Yet just when it looked like Jerusalem was set for a long siege, Richard once again pulled his forces back, resolving another difficult debate amongst the Christian nobles about the viability of prosecuting a siege and of administrating and holding the city should it be captured.

Saladin, encouraged by Richard's second pullback from Jerusalem, attacked and seized the city of Jaffa (Christian soldiers and citizens still held the citadel) after a four-day siege. In one of the boldest counter-strokes, however, Richard sailed up the coast and launched an audacious amphibious attack with 54 knights, soon supported by 2000 Italian crossbowmen. Saladin's forces were disordered by the boldness of the move and defeated by the fighting skills of the English knights and the endless accurate Italian crossbow fire. Both sides were now almost spent, the armies on both sides exhausted by war, casualties and constant marching. Saladin and Richard therefore opted for diplomacy to settle the conflict. The Treaty of Jaffa was signed on 2 September. Through this instrument, the two opposing leaders agreed a three-year truce, with Saladin retaining control of Jerusalem but agreeing the free passage of pilgrims to the Christian holy sites in the city. The crusaders were permitted to hold on to Acre and Jaffa, and the coastal strip between, but Ascalon was once again to be destroyed.

The Treaty of Jaffa was a rather damp and ignominious end to the Third Crusade, its weary pragmatics a long way from the aspirations with which it started. For the crusaders, it once again showed the challenge of holding a large, multinational army together in times of political and social complexity, and the uphill struggle to defeat the established armies of Islam. Not that Saladin was exactly covered in glory either. His military prestige had been dented by several Christian victories, plus he was slowly slipping into serious illness. The great Saladin died on 3 March 1193, at the age of 55.

As for Richard, his return journey was every bit as eventful as his outgoing journey. Trying to evade his many European enemies by travelling disguised, badly as it turned out, as a monk, he was captured by Duke Leopold V of Austria just before Christmas 1192 near Vienna, and imprisoned and put up for ransom. He would not be released until February 1194 (Philip and John ensured a slow release) for the sum of 150,000 silver marks, having his crown reinstated in April. Richard I died of gangrene on 6 April 1199, following a crossbow injury received during a siege of the Château de Chalus-Chabrol in southern France. He remained a warrior until the very end.

Below: Richard I is recognized and captured in Vienna during his return to Europe from the Third Crusade.

5

THE FOURTH CRUSADE

Amongst a field of strong contenders, the Fourth Crusade surely stands as the nadir of the crusading era. Through a dark sequence of mismanagement and political manoeuvring, not only did the crusaders never even reach the Holy Land, they also ultimately directed all of their violent energies upon attacking Christian communities, culminating in the violent massacres within Constantinople itself.

By the end of the twelfth century, crusading to the Holy Land had almost become as much of a cultural phenomenon as a political one. The ethical code of chivalry, which had been progressively codifying itself since the late eleventh century, provided fertile soil in which to sow the seeds of crusading aspirations, especially when combined with the constant religious manoeuvring of the medieval world. Nevertheless, state rulers were showing an increased reluctance to getting involved with the practicalities of crusading, having now seen the financial, political and military risks of these long-distance campaigns.

Opposite: The great Venetian artist Tintoretto captures the drama of the fall of Constantinople to Frankish forces in 1204, in a catastrophic reversal of the original spirit of the Crusades.

The Fourth Crusade was to be, at least in its original form, a campaign very much under the control and direction of the papacy. In August 1138, Pope Innocent III, fired principally by the conviction that Muslim rule over the Holy City of Jerusalem was unacceptable, made new calls for a Crusade. There was also an opportunistic sideline here, however. In March 1195 in Constantinople, a new Byzantine Emperor was crowned: Alexios III Angelos. His path to power was unsavoury, although not wholly uncharacteristic of the age. He had deposed, blinded and imprisoned his younger brother, Emperor Isaac II Angelos, along with his son, Prince Alexios. This evident cruelty was rather less important to the Pope than Prince Alexios' interest in the possibility of unifying the Greek and Latin churches under Rome. Such a dramatic expansion and consolidation of the Pope's power would doubtless have formed a strong undercurrent in Innocent III's strategic interests in the Middle East.

INNOCENT ALSO PERMITTED WEALTHY INDIVIDUALS TO FUND PEOPLE TO TAKE THE CROSS ON THEIR BEHALF, WITH ALL THE SAME HEAVENLY BENEFITS FOR THE DONOR.

Below: Pope Innocent III was consumed by his desire to restore the Holy Land to Christian control, making him out of touch with political and military realities.

CALLING FOR THE CRUSADE

In the autumn, Innocent made his call for a Crusade public. He did so with a greater emphasis on discipline than many previous Popes. Authorized preachers were approved, avoiding rabble-rousing populists, and they used more restrained language, while also stating that any crusaders had to take the cross for two years minimum – the flaky or uncommitted were thereby discouraged. These measures were taken to avoid the mad rush of fervent but ineffective civilians to the Crusade. Yet Innocent still wanted to support or hire poorer but proficient men-at-arms, so while the nobility would still have to be self-funding, a new church income tax would pay for the others. In one further twist on raising an army, Innocent also permitted wealthy individuals to fund people to take the cross on their behalf, with all the same heavenly benefits for the donor.

The call for the Crusade spread out across Europe, but the response was less than sparkling. Europe's

CHIVALRY

Left: In this medieval illumination, a Knight Templar pays tribute to his king – the concept of loyalty to one's rulers, even unto death, was central to chivalric codes.

MEDIEVAL CHIVALRY WAS A multi-layered ethical system, one that not only came to evoke martial bravery and feudal loyalty, but also, with time and literary embellishment, an air of romanticism. The word itself derives from the French words *cheval* (horse) and *chevalier* (knight), and in its earliest form it was basically an unwritten code of honour for high-ranking knights, one that laid down expectations of behaviour such as loyalty (very important in a feudal era) and bravery, dignity in behaviour and morality in action. By following such standards, furthermore, the knights could also distinguish themselves from the common man; chivalry was as much about feudal hierarchies as it was about human decency. The Church was naturally keen to tie chivalry's good intentions to its own purposes, thus chivalry also came to include a sense of Christian duty, particularly in the defence of the Christian faith, its institutions and its people. Needless to say, this sort of morality could be conveniently strapped to the purposes of a Crusade.

Chivalry was sharpened in the public mind by a growing volume of literature, prose, poetry and songs, which eulogized and mythologized the chivalrous knight, particularly through the telling of the legend of King Arthur and his knights of the Round Table. Literary chivalry embedded notions of courtly love (generally unrequited) and sexual purity amongst the military valour, which was in itself heightened by tales of knights doing battle with all manner of evil, from wicked foreigners to terrifying dragons. Outside the realms of fiction, knights could also visibly demonstrate their chivalric qualities on the tournament field; the medieval tournament, with its jousts and melees, established themselves from the twelfth century. Chivalry became codified in manuals, such as *Book of the Order of Chivalry* by Aragonian Ramon Llull (1265) and the *Book of Chivalry* by Geoffroi de Charny (c. 1350). Although the expectations of chivalry undoubtedly guided some behaviour for the better, the history of the later Crusades illustrates how the concepts could be a long way from the reality.

great powers, having in recent memory participated in a costly and ultimately fruitless Crusade, had little incentive to join another. Furthermore, previous combatants such as Richard I and Philip II were too busy fighting each other to vacate their kingdoms and fight elsewhere. The Holy Roman Empire was in the midst of a succession crisis, and one with uncertain outcomes for Europe and the papacy; Innocent was reluctant to involve the ambitious contenders.

Opposite: Pope Innocent III blesses crusaders in Saint Mark's Basilica, Venice, Italy in 1202. Despite Innocent's strengthening of the papacy, his ultimate control over the crusaders proved limited.

Thus the Pope had to tap into other wellsprings of recruitment. At a major tournament in Écry, Champagne, in November 1199, the Crusade was proclaimed again, this time in front of a crowd of knights and lords, doubtless keen to make a public display of virtue. The host of the event, Count Thibaut (Theobald) III of Champagne, took the cross, and was followed by nobles such as Count Louis of Blois, Simon de Montfort (a French noble and the English 6th Earl of Leicester), Count Baldwin IX of Flanders/VI of Hainault (who would supply the largest combat component of the Fourth Crusade) and Geoffrey de Villehardouin, the Marshal of Champagne. Thus Pope Innocent now had his crusading army. He would not control it for long.

VENETIAN INPUT

Actual planning for the campaign that lay ahead was conducted by the senior nobles, who made little effort to seek the counsel of the Pope. In fact, hidden agendas were emerging. The most critical decision was to make Egypt, and specifically Cairo, the first objective of the Fourth Crusade. As historians have noted, there was some strategic sense in this decision. Saladin's Egypt was undoubtedly the centre of Muslim power in the Middle East at this time; if Egypt could be taken, then recapturing Jerusalem could be accomplished with far greater confidence. There was also enormous wealth in Egypt; financial gain was always a strong motivator for nobles about to embark on a costly military Crusade. Yet at the same time, on an ideological level the diversion to Egypt would be a hard sell for those who were spiritually motivated by the focus on Jerusalem. For this reason, the

Below: Enrico Dandolo, the aged, blind, but quick-witted Doge of Venice, manipulated the Fourth Crusade to suit his own political purposes.

senior nobles kept this information not only from the crusaders themselves – they would be told off the shores of Egypt – but also from the Pope. It was now clear who was running the show.

The main problem now was how to get there. Unlike past Crusades, the option of marching overland was not on the table. Thus the Fourth Crusade would be a maritime expedition. Having no fleet of their own, the crusader nobles turned to Venice – one of the greatest naval and commercial powers in Europe at this time – to provide the requisite shipping. In the spring of 1201, Villehardouin and five other deputies embarked on negotiations with the doge (ruler of Venice), Enrico Dandolo. Dandolo was 90 years old, but he remained an intellectually vital individual, and a shrewd operator when it came to contractual and political discussions. His one significant physical problem, near blindness, in no way dulled his acumen. An agreement was finally reached. Venice would provide shipping for a crusader force of 33,500 men, plus nine-months of associated logistics and supplies. (Specifically, Venice committed itself to providing, per person, roughly three litres by volume of flour, grain and vegetables and a half amphora of wine, plus around 25 litres of fodder for an estimated 1500 horses.)

THE AGREEMENT WAS FOR THE CRUSADERS TO PAY 85,000 MARKS IN CASH PLUS 50 PER CENT OF ALL THE PLUNDER OR RICHES.

Although Venice possessed an extensive merchant navy, the scale of the adventure meant more ships were required, so the deal struck between the Venetians and the crusaders included a major shipbuilding programme. None of this was going to be cheap. The agreement was for the crusaders to pay 85,000 marks in cash plus 50 per cent of all the plunder or riches obtained during the Crusade. It was a good outcome for the doge, but one that would come back to haunt the crusaders. Furthermore, the Pope had not been involved in the discussions – he was only informed about the terms and conditions once they were signed.

DEPARTURE AND DIVERSION

From mid 1202, the crusading army steadily began to accumulate in Venice. But the gap between signing the shipping agreement

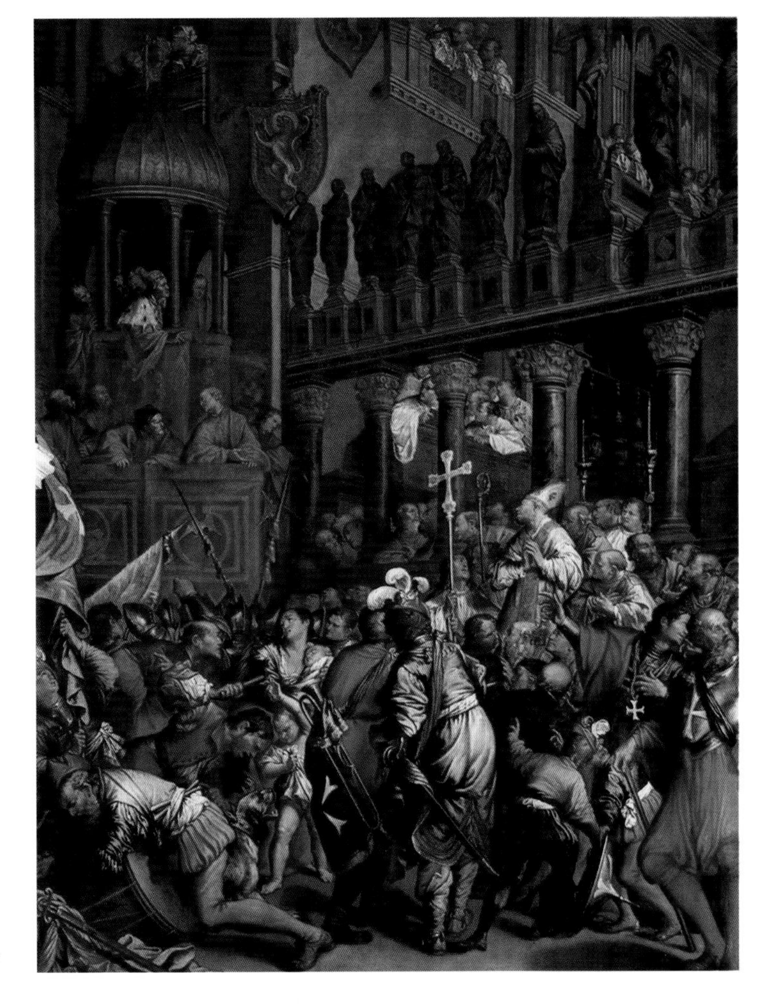

Above: The Venetian doge Enrico Dandolo recruits troops for the Fourth Crusade, in scenes that depict religious passion bordering on chaos.

and the actual launch of the Crusade was a long one, a space in which many people could ruminate on their decision or be distracted by other matters in life. It was a necessary space – Venice had to construct a new fleet of 50 armed galleys – but it had a critical effect on the military manpower. In total, it is estimated that fewer than half of the 33,500 men actually presented themselves for service when the time came. In terms of the Venetian deal, a serious problem was now emerging. The Crusade was relying upon the wealth of the participants to cover the cost of 85,000 marks; with too few people turning up, there was simply not enough money to pay the doge (only 51,000 marks was collected). The issue was compounded by the fact that a significant number of crusaders had found independent means of shipping out to the Holy Land on a schedule that suited them.

Until the money, or some other solution, could be found, the Crusade was stuck – the soldiers who had turned up were camped offshore on Lido island, becoming increasingly frustrated. It was the doge who hit on a solution. He proposed that full payment to Venice could come after completion of the Crusade, but with one very specific condition. Dandolo wanted the crusaders to help him capture the city of Zara (modern Zadar) in Croatia. This Christian city, which had formerly been a Venetian dependency, had pledged its allegiance to King Imre of Hungary, rather than to Venice, in 1182. Not seeing a way around the financial issues, the crusading nobles agreed. Furthermore, the doge now took the cross himself, and added a force of 21,000 men to the campaign – Venice was now essentially in control of the Crusade.

Below: The crusaders storm the city of Zara in 1202, an act for which they earned an excommunication from Pope Innocent III.

The political fallout of the Zara decision was profound. Morale plunged amongst the French and Flemish crusaders; they had taken the cross to fight Muslims, not fellow Christians. Furthermore, King Imre had actually taken the cross himself, something that the doge disregarded as a false display of piety rather than an actual commitment to fight. When the Pope found out about the plan, he forbade it, but the doge prevented any papal instructions from reaching the fleet, which sailed on 1 October.

Zara was a powerful city, but the combined crusader/Venetian army totalled more than 20,000 men, embarked in some 210 warships and carrying more than 300 siege engines of various kinds. Zara came under siege on 10 November and on 24 November the city capitulated, and was subsequently destroyed and plundered.

Once he heard this news, Pope Innocent III was furious. He excommunicated both the Franks and the Venetians. The Crusade was cancelled, and Pope Innocent insisted that King Imre be fully compensated. He berated the crusaders as follows: 'See how your gold has become base metal and your silver has almost completely rusted away since you deviated from the purity of your plan and turned aside from the true path onto the impassable road. You have, so to speak, taken your hand from the plough ... When ... you should have gone straight to the land flowing with milk and honey, you turned away, going astray in the desert.'

The French crusaders quickly repented of their wrongdoing, to the extent that Innocent reinstated them in the Church and confirmed the Crusade, although he forbade further interaction between Franks and Venetians. It was now, however, that fate intervened once again, taking the Crusade in the direction that few could have conceived as possible.

OBJECTIVE – CONSTANTINOPLE

In 1202, Prince Alexios – the son of the blinded and deposed Emperor Isaac – managed to escape his captivity in Constantinople and made his way to the west. Prince Alexios was keen to see his cruel uncle deposed and Isaac returned to the throne, for which he needed external assistance. Yet he knew that neither the papacy nor nobles would be persuaded purely by ethical arguments. So, building on the fact that a crusading army was already fairly close by, Prince Alexios made a startling proposal to major figures in the Crusade – particularly Duke Philip of Swabia and Boniface of Montferrat. He proposed that if the crusaders could restore his father to rule, then the Byzantine Empire would place the Orthodox Church under the authority of the Western Popes, thereby uniting the Greek and Latin faiths, with Rome in charge. As if this wasn't attractive enough for the crusaders, Prince Alexios also pledged to provide the Crusade with an additional 10,000 troops plus 200,000 silver marks and a year's worth of supplies.

PRINCE ALEXIOS ALSO PLEDGED TO PROVIDE THE CRUSADE WITH AN ADDITIONAL 10,000 TROOPS PLUS 200,000 SILVER MARKS AND A YEAR'S WORTH OF SUPPLIES.

For key figures in the crusading army, many of whom already had antithetical relationships with the Byzantine Empire, and who were still heavily indebted to Venice, the offer seemed too good to turn down. They would have known the repercussions. Pope Innocent, as part of reinstating the Franks after their excommunication, had made them swear that they would not attack any further Christian cities during the Crusade. Clearly, the temptation of taking Constantinople itself overrode such considerations. Venice's involvement broke another of the Pope's conditions, and indeed the Venetian participation would be essential. A significant number of the original crusaders left when they heard of the new plan, losing faith with the enterprise. Pope Innocent even sent a letter forbidding the action, but this arrived after the main fleet had set sail, with their new purpose, on 20 April 1203.

THE ATTACK ON CONSTANTINOPLE

The journey to Constantinople was an ill-tempered one. The first port of call was the island of Corfu, where there were further heated debates about whether to direct the Crusade towards Egypt or Constantinople. There were also significant supply problems, with chronic shortages of food. But the focus on Constantinople remained. Prince Alexios, who also went to Corfu, assured the crusaders that the city would quickly capitulate, as the loyalty to Alexios III was fragile.

The fleet set sail from Corfu on 24 May 1203 and thereafter wound its way around the southern Balkans, across the Aegean Sea, through the Dardanelles and into the Sea of Marmara. They eventually arrived at Agios Stefanos, just a short distance from

Below: This painting by Vasilios Chatzis (1870–1915) shows the Venetian fleet assaulting the walls of Constantinople directly from the sea.

Above: A miniature from the *Historia* by William of Tyre shows the fleet of the Fourth Crusade setting sail

Constantinople, on 23 June. In the Bosphoros, Alexios III made his first, rather feeble, attempt to restrain the invaders militarily, when he positioned a substantial force of cavalry and infantry on the shoreline. Yet courage failed them that day, and as the crusaders headed to shore the Greeks quickly melted away, and retreated back behind the city walls.

The crusading army had nowhere near the manpower to place Constantinople under a wrap-around siege. Instead, it essentially divided itself into two parts. The mainly French crusaders made a landward attack against the Genoese quarter, Galata. There was a large tower there, which served as the northern anchor point for a huge defensive boom, 750m (2460ft) long, that stretched across the entrance to the Golden Horn, a wide estuary that formed the north-eastern border to Constantinople. Meanwhile, the Venetian army remained aboard ships, using the vessels as firing platforms for crossbows, archery and ship-mounted stone-throwing machines (an early example of offshore naval bombardment) and waiting for the moment to make an amphibious assault once the boom could be taken down.

Below: Crusaders in boats arrive at the walls of Constantinople during the Fourth Crusade. About 200 ships were employed in the assault.

The Galata Tower was bombarded relentlessly by boulders, arrows and other missiles, and its defenders simply could not hold out. It was stormed and taken by the crusaders on 6 July. The boom was unhooked from its anchor point, and now the Venetian ships could penetrate into the Golden Horn, attacking the ships of the Byzantine fleet that mostly lay helplessly at anchor. Fireships were used to burn up many of these vessels.

To continue their attack, the crusaders now focused their attentions on the north-west corner of the defences, setting up a siege camp opposite the Blachernae Palace, a major imperial

CROSSBOWS

ALTHOUGH THE CROSSBOW WAS an ancient weapon, the hand-held crossbow was only adopted widely in medieval armies from the late twelfth and early thirteenth centuries. The basic crossbow consisted of a wooden stock, grooved to take a short wooden bolt and fitted with a horn, wood, iron or steel bow, strung with inelastic hemp. The draw weight of the bow was considerable; basic hand-cocked crossbows could have a draw weight of about 68kg (150lb) up to extremely powerful versions with draw weights exceeding 454kg (1000lb). The varying powers produced ranges of anywhere between 100 and 350m (328 and 1148ft), and as the weights increased various mechanical devices, particularly windlasses, had to be used to make cocking possible. The crossbow was in some ways inferior to the conventional longbow, which could achieve similar ranges but with a far faster rate of fire. A trained archer could unleash as many as 12 arrows per minute, whereas a crossbowman typically averaged about two bolts in the same time. Yet a crossbow could be operated convincingly by a relatively untrained man (an archer took many years to reach proficiency), the flat line-of-sight arrangement making accurate sighted shooting a possibility. The heavy, stubby crossbow bolt could also punch through many types of medieval armour, thus the crossbow-armed infantryman was a very real threat to the mail- and plate-clad knight. Much like the firearms that began their evolution in Europe in the thirteenth century, crossbows were a great battlefield leveller and force multiplier.

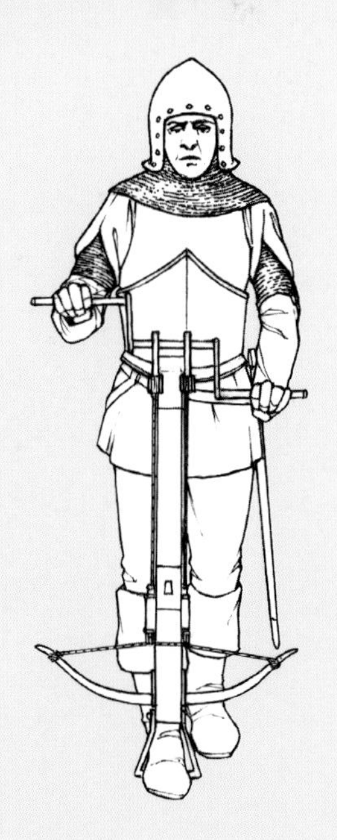

Above: This crossbowman spans the bow using a metal claw attached to a leather strap around the waist.

Left: This crossbow is spanned using a 'goat's hook' lever, to apply mechanical advantage.

Right: For the most powerful crossbows, a windlass system was used, giving a mechanical advantage of up to 30:1.

Byzantine residence. There then followed about a week of missile exchanges against and over the walls, punctuated by the occasional cavalry charge and infantry assault, albeit without a conclusive result. The Venetians made a particularly skilful use of their craft, which moved in close to towers that bordered the water, and took many of them with assaults directly off the decks using assault ladders and grappling hooks, these often being rigged to the ships' masts to give them elevation and precision positioning.

Alexios III sensed his grip on the Byzantine capital slipping. He pushed back with a major cavalry deployment, but after much confused manoeuvring the action fizzled out and the Byzantines pulled back. The problems for the defenders were compounded by a huge fire that was started by incendiary attacks, the blaze raging out of control and eventually destroying a large part of the city.

THE FALL AND THE MASSACRE

On 17 July 1203, Constantinople finally fell to the crusaders, with Alexios III fleeing the city that night. Immediately Isaac was freed from his imprisonment, and he took his throne again, this time beside Prince Alexios; the two men serving as co-emperors: Alexios IV and Isaac II. The Pope, still fuming over his total loss of control over the Crusade, instructed the crusaders to commit themselves to their original purpose, a campaign in the Holy Land, but that focus was now leaking out of the campaign. Instead, the crusaders and Constantinople's population sat together in an atmosphere of increasing tension and mistrust. Riots broke out, with violence directed towards some of the Latin quarters of the city, and a more organized Byzantine resistance began to flare up, there even being efforts to destroy the Venetian shipping in the harbour. It also looked increasingly likely that Alexios IV was going to struggle to pay the monies that he had promised; he even resorted to melting down precious objects from Constantinople's churches, in an effort to raise revenue.

RIOTS BROKE OUT, WITH VIOLENCE DIRECTED TOWARDS SOME OF THE LATIN QUARTERS OF THE CITY, AND A MORE ORGANIZED BYZANTINE RESISTANCE BEGAN TO FLARE UP...

Matters were reaching boiling point. In November 1203, Alexios IV finally stopped paying his debts to the crusaders, and fell out publicly with the doge. Here was a dangerous moment for Alexios IV, as the doge was essentially no friend of the Byzantine Empire – he perceived it as a major competitor with Venice for maritime and commercial supremacy in the region – plus large numbers of Constantinople's citizens and nobles were turning against him, for what they saw as his courting an enemy. The leader of the anti-Latin movement, the noble Alexios Doukas Mourtzouphlos, then mounted a coup, seizing power on 25 January 1204 and proclaiming himself Alexios V. Alexios IV was murdered and Isaac II died of grief and age shortly after.

It was now that the Fourth Crusade took the ugliest of turns. The crusaders and Venetians decided together to suppress Constantinople by force, and without much in the way of mercy

Above: For the taking of Constantinople, many of the Venetian ships had been specially adapted so that the crusaders could assault the walls straight from the decks.

Right: A depiction of Alexios IV Angelos being crowned co-emperor alongside his father Isaac II, on 1 August 1203. His reign would last a mere six months, and would end in his murder on 8 February 1204.

or restraint. The French crusading knight Robert de Clari has usefully left us an eyewitness account of this time, and here he explains the theological and ethical gymnastics performed by the nobles and the clergy to release the dogs of war against what was still one of the greatest centres of Christendom in the world:

> *LXXII. When the pilgrims saw this, they were very angry and grieved much; they went back from the other side of the harbour to their lodgings. When the barons had returned and had gotten ashore, they assembled and were much amazed, and said that it was on account of their sins that they did not succeed in anything and could not capture the city. Meanwhile the bishops and the clergy in the army debated and decided that the war was a righteous one, and they certainly ought to attack the Greeks. For formerly the inhabitants of the city had been obedient to the law of Rome and now they were disobedient, since they said that the law of Rome was of no account, and called all who believed in it 'dogs'. And the bishop said that for this reason one ought certainly to attack them, and that it was not a sin, but an act of great charity. Then it was announced to all the host that all the Venetians and everyone else should go and hear the sermons on Sunday morning and they did so. Then the bishops preached to the*

> *army . . . and they showed to the pilgrims that the war was a righteous one; for the Greeks were traitors and murderers, and also disloyal, since they had murdered their rightful lord, and were worse than Jews. Moreover, the bishops said that, by the authority of God and in the name of the Pope, they would absolve all who attacked the Greeks.*

The crusaders were at this time based across the Golden Horn from the city; Alexios IV had insisted that the main army camped across the river. On 9 April, having embarked aboard their ships the previous day, the crusaders made the assault across the estuary, assaulting the Golden Horn fortifications while facing a barrage of fire from Byzantine engines. By 12 April, the attackers had managed to gain lodgements on the city's walls then pushed inside, forcing Alexios V to flee that night. (He was later captured and blinded.)

CONSTANTINOPLE FINALLY CAPITULATED TO THE CRUSADERS THE NEXT DAY, 13 APRIL. THERE NOW COMMENCED THREE DAYS OF THE MOST WANTON DESTRUCTION AND MURDER.

Constantinople finally capitulated to the crusaders the next day, 13 April. There now commenced three days of the most wanton destruction and murder, the crusaders looking to punish those who resisted them, and virtually given theological licence to do so. The city was stripped of its valuables on an epic scale, treasures of every conceivable type being taken forcibly from churches, monasteries, palaces and civic buildings, and usually ending up decorating buildings back in Western Europe. (The four bronze horses that sit on the façade of St Mark's Basilica, Venice, are a particularly famous example, although today they are replicas.) There was also horrific and vengeful bloodletting. Robert de Clari captures something of the human darkness:

> *No one was without a share in the grief. In the alleys, in the streets, in the temples, complaints, weeping, lamentations, grief, the groaning of men, the shrieks of women, wounds, rape, captivity, the separation of those most closely united. Nobles wandered about ignominiously, those of venerable*

age in tears, the rich in poverty. Thus it was in the streets, on the corners, in the temple, in the dens, for no place remained unassailed or defended the suppliants. All places everywhere were filled full of all kinds of crime. Oh, immortal God, how great the afflictions of the men, how great the distress!

Opposite: A relief icon of the Archangel St Michael, worked into plate armour. Thousands of items such as these were looted from Constantinople, and were subsequently traded on the elite markets of Europe.

Eventually the destruction subsided, although reports of it would later convulse the Western world. Now the crusaders set to work, in their typically divided and back-biting way, to establish the new feudal and religious hierarchy over Constantinople. Baldwin of Flanders, much to the disappointment of Boniface of Montferrat, was appointed the new Emperor, and even received papal blessing several weeks later; while the takeover of Constantinople had by no means been the Pope's original intention, there were now de facto reasons for Innocent III to embrace the arrangement. A Latin Patriarch of Constantinople was also appointed, Thomas Morosini, a Venetian priest. In fact, Venice and its doge did particularly well out of the conquest of the Byzantine Empire, which was labelled 'Romania'. Crete and Corfu passed to Venetian control, and Venice also took charge of commercial activity in Constantinople itself.

The Fourth Crusade now came to its effective conclusion, the crusaders mostly returning home. They had fought only Christians, had not set foot in the Holy Land or Egypt, had destroyed the Byzantine Empire and had achieved all this mostly without the direction or blessing of the Pope, who had initiated the Crusade in the first place. Moreover, the sack of Constantinople established enmities between East and West that in some corners of the continent have lingered to this very day. It is hard to envision how the Fourth Crusade could have been further from the ideals and objectives of the First Crusade a century earlier.

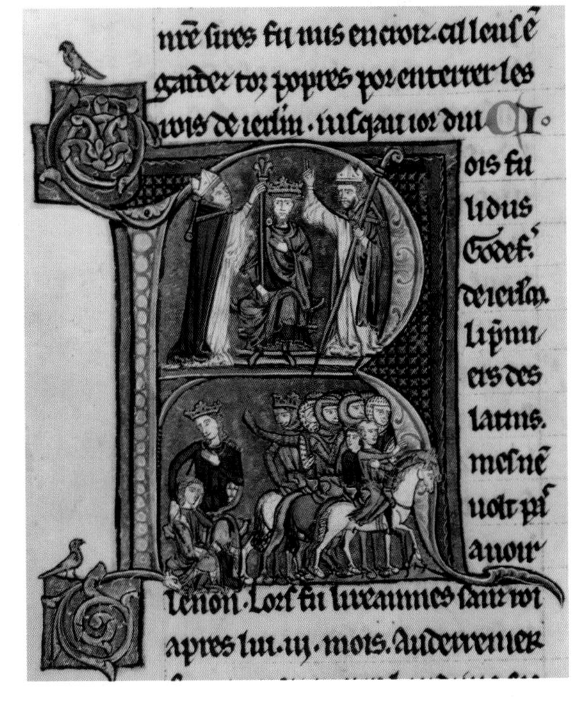

Below: An illumination of Baldwin I of Flanders being crowned in what was now the Latin Empire of Constantinople. The city was reconquered by the Byzantines in 1261.

6

CRUSADES IN WESTERN AND NORTHERN EUROPE

The Holy Land was to remain the spiritual focus of the crusading philosophy throughout the medieval period. Control of that territory, however, progressively passed into the hands of Muslim rule, never to be reclaimed. This effect, combined with the political, commercial and religious incentives, meant that many of Europe's knights and warriors did not need to journey overseas to wage war on the infidels.

Opposite: A Teutonic Knight depicted in an ornate and colourful mosaic in Cologne Cathedral, Germany.

BY THE TWELFTH CENTURY, crusading had become, for Europe's warrior classes, as much a way of life as an occasional practice. Indeed, although the Fourth Crusade ended in relative ignominy, the religious appetite for crusading remained alive and well, a force that

Europe's leaders could tap into when they felt the urge or necessity. What had changed, as we shall see in the next chapter, was a higher degree of practical reticence amongst monarchs, nobles and Popes (some, not all) to get involved in further expensive and uncertain campaigns for what many felt was increasingly a lost cause.

Nevertheless, the crusading spirit was a flexible one. While the Crusades began with a usefully definable enemy – the Muslim world – the Fourth Crusade in particular had shown that other peoples, even Christians (and always Jews), could become additional and unfortunate targets. Anyone who practised a non-Christian belief system, such as pagans, or who expounded a version of Christianity deemed heretical or non-aligned with Catholic doctrine, could be potentially defined as an enemy of Christendom. Taking this broad perspective meant that there was a wider spectrum of crusading opportunities than the long-winded and likely disastrous transit to the Holy Land. Instead, the swords of the crusaders could be brought to bear on peoples far closer to home.

THE IBERIAN PENINSULA

Looking at Western Europe in general, an on-the-doorstep objective for crusaders was the Iberian peninsula, which had largely fallen under Muslim Moorish rule in the eighth century. There was intermittent fighting between Moors and Christians in Iberia for many centuries following, but a distinctive and unplanned incursion there actually formed part of the Second Crusade.

ALL SEEMED TO BE GOING TO PLAN, BUT DURING THE PASSAGE AROUND THE IBERIAN PENINSULA THE CRUSADING FLEET STRUCK A PATCH OF FEROCIOUS WEATHER.

In 1147, the British component of the Second Crusade, headed by men such as Hervey de Glanville (the Constable of Suffolk, and the major commanding figure of the expedition), Simon of Dover, Master Andrew of London, and William and Ralph Veal, intended on taking the southern maritime route to the Holy Land. It should be noted that although the army would sail from England, it was actually thoroughly international in composition. The largest component was certainly the English, who numbered perhaps 6000 men, but there were also an estimated 5000 Germans (particularly Rhinelanders led by Arnout IV, Count of Aarschot) and 2000 Flemings. They embarked on a fleet of some 164 ships, sailing from the southern port of Dartmouth, the numbers of vessels swelling as they tracked down the coastline of Brittany, perhaps to as many as 200.

All seemed to be going to plan, but during the passage around the Iberian Peninsula the crusading fleet struck a patch of ferocious weather, and they were forced to land

Left: The Alhambra Palace in Granada, Spain, was centre of Moorish rule until the Christian reconquest of the city in 1492. Elements of its Islamic decoration remain to this day.

Above: The siege of Lisbon, 1147. A mighty Christian siege tower is drawn manually up to the walls of the city. Note the shield wall protecting those pushing the tower.

in Oporto in modern Portugal, on the border of Muslim and Christian territories. Oporto's Portuguese (Christian) ruler was Count Afonso Henriques, a man whose nascent kingdom sat in an awkward position between the Christian states to the north and east and the Moorish rule to the south. Up until 1139, the county of Portugal had been ruled by the medieval Spanish Kingdom of Leon. Leon's emperor, Alfonso VI, had granted practical rule of Portugal to Henry of Burgundy, Afonso's father, and Henry dutifully led Portugal throughout turbulent years against Muslim incursions. The relationship between Portugal and Leon was cemented by Henry's marriage to Alfonso's illegitimate daughter, Teresa. When Henry died in 1112, however, the heir to the throne – Afonso – was but two years old, so Teresa stepped in as his guardian and the de facto ruler of

Portugal. It was a position she came to enjoy, so much so that she didn't want to relinquish it when Afonso came of age, resulting in a civil war for the future of the state. The deciding battle took place on 24 June 1128, at São Mamede near Guimarães, when forces led by Afonso decisively defeated those of Teresa and her lover Fernão Peres de Trava. Following the clash, Afonso declared himself Prince of Portugal, although he was initially regarded as a vassal of Alfonso VII of Leon, his cousin. Then in 1139 Afonso took the decisive step away from Spanish control, taking the title King of Portugal.

WHEN A LARGE CRUSADING ARMY WASHED UP ON HIS SHORES, THEREFORE, AFONSO SENSED AN OPPORTUNITY TO HELP CEMENT THE SECURITY OF HIS KINGDOM.

When a large crusading army washed up on his shores, therefore, Afonso sensed an opportunity to help cement the security of his kingdom, both by expanding the amount of territory under Portuguese rule and by demonstrating Portuguese independence, in emphatic military fashion, to the Spanish and to the papacy. In fact, Portugal was already actively warring against its Muslim neighbours at this time. At the battle of Ourique on 25 July 1139, for example, Afonso's army inflicted a major defeat upon the forces of the Almoravid dynasty, led by Ali ibn Yusuf, and Afonso (at this point still a prince) was able to impose tribute payments on the Muslims. In the summer of 1140 or 1141, it was time for Christian to fight Christian, as Afonso and Alfonso VII came to blows at the battle of Valdevez, brought about initially over a typically medieval dispute over who should succeed to Alfonso's throne, but which then became a war to confirm Portuguese independence. Afonso took the important victory, but by 1147, when the crusaders arrived, Afonso still felt the need to extend and secure his kingdom. He therefore argued that the crusaders could serve both their religious impulses and their baser desire for bounty by helping him to reclaim the city of Lisbon to the south, which had been under Muslim rule since 711.

The crusader leadership was ultimately convinced by Afonso's arguments, the wheels likely oiled by the fact that Afonso promised the crusaders that they could take any moveable goods they found in the city. Also, here was a potential opportunity for the crusaders to maintain their military pilgrimage without travelling for additional months; after all, they were still fighting Muslims.

Thus, the crusaders turned south and Lisbon was placed under siege on 1 July 1147. The crusading force quickly cut off all supplies running into the fortified city, and established a defendable perimeter against any possible relief army. The crusaders also thumped Lisbon's walls and buildings with the missiles of siege engines, plus built siege towers in readiness for the final assault. The siege dragged on for 17 weeks, and as one of the Christian siege towers finally came up to the very base of the walls, the now-starving inhabitants of Lisbon judiciously surrendered on 21 October. Gilbert of Hastings, an English monk and member of the Christian army, was subsequently appointed as the first Bishop of Lisbon. While some of the crusaders now embarked on vessels for the Holy Land, intent on prosecuting the campaign as originally envisaged, many of them felt that they had now played their part, and actually began new lives as permanent inhabitants of the city. Lisbon would become the capital of Portugal in 1255.

Over the next 350 years, Iberia was progressively reclaimed for Christendom, principally by Spanish armies, but also with some assistance from the Military Orders. Although the Christian states, particularly those of the kingdoms of Aragon, Castile and Portugal, did suffer some signal setbacks, such as the massive defeat at the battle of Alarcos on 18 July 1195, the momentum against the Moors steadily grew apace. Cordoba fell in 1236, Seville in 1248 and Cadiz in 1262, but it was not until 1492 that Granada in the far south was finally taken and the remnants of the Muslim presence expelled from the peninsula. The *Reconquista*, as we now call the reconquest of Spain and Portugal from the Moors, was not a Crusade in itself, but as the siege of Lisbon had demonstrated, it certainly sat comfortably with the crusading age.

IT WAS NOT UNTIL 1492 THAT GRANADA IN THE FAR SOUTH WAS FINALLY TAKEN AND THE REMNANTS OF THE MUSLIM PRESENCE EXPELLED FROM THE PENINSULA.

Left: The 'Children's Crusade' was a strange moment in the history of the Crusades. Some have argued that it was Europe's first youth movement.

THE CHILDREN'S AND SHEPHERDS' CRUSADES

In terms of the overarching objectives of the Crusades, the reconquest of the Iberian peninsula had a definite logic. But the crusading ethos was equally capable of launching stranger and more riotous acts, such as the impromptu anti-Semitic violence we have seen in previous chapters. One of the most curious examples of crusader spontaneity, however, is that of the so-called Children's Crusade of 1212.

The imaginative popularization of crusading meant that it was not only the wealthy and noble strata of society that were inspired to acts of religious militarism. In early 1212, a

German teenager, Nicholas of Cologne, reportedly received a divine vision, telling him to lead a Crusade to free the Holy Land, God even reassuring him that the waters of the Mediterranean would be parted by divine fiat when they reached them, enabling the crusaders to walk to their destination. The movement around Nicholas grew apace, and within months he had an unconventional army of thousands of common people from all walks of life, and including a large number of children and adolescents. (Although the Children's Crusade

Below: The Shepherds' Crusade of 1251 had a bucolic name, but it was characterized by random violence – here the bodies of victims swing from the trees.

has naturally been identified with its youth element, there was a large percentage – probably a majority – of adults in the army, not least many of the parents of the children.) A similar movement was ignited in France in May 1212, by a shepherd boy, Stephen of Cloyes, who even received an audience with the king of France, Philip II Augustus, who praised his spirit but recommended he go home, advice that the spiritually entranced Stephen chose to ignore. Stephen's army may have eventually numbered up to 30,000 people.

The outcome of the Children's Crusade is rather sadly predictable. The two immense columns suffered the grinding attrition of hunger, thirst, exposure, banditry and sheer exhaustion. Many of the children ended up being virtual prisoners of the unscrupulous and exploitative peoples they passed on the way, becoming nothing more than household slaves. Yet many still crossed the Alps and even reached Mediterranean coastal ports, but there they were confronted by a sea that remained obstinately closed to foot traffic. After several weeks of forlorn waiting, the dispirited remnants of the Children's Crusade eventually dispersed.

THE TWO IMMENSE COLUMNS SUFFERED THE GRINDING ATTRITION OF HUNGER, THIRST, EXPOSURE, BANDITRY AND SHEER EXHAUSTION.

Some 40 years later, in 1251, there was another impromptu and unauthorized (by the Pope) commoner's Crusade, this time known as the Shepherds' Crusade. A resident of Picardy (likely Amiens), a monk called Master Jacob of Hungary, claimed to have received a divine commission from the Virgin Mary, telling him to lead an army of *pastoreaux* ('shepherds', but essentially any peasant or land worker) to the Holy Land to assist the French king, Louis IX, who had been captured by the Egyptians (see next chapter).

It was said that his army eventually numbered 60,000, doubtless an exaggeration but an indicator of strength, and they marched first to Paris and then south to Orléans and then Bourges. On the way, the 'army' revealed itself as nothing more than a thuggish mob, given to spontaneous acts of violence and criminality. Some of this was directed against a familiar 'enemy', the Jews, but there was also the destruction and desecration of churches and aggression towards the clergy. Indeed, the movement showed a strong anticlericalism, but it had little discipline, doctrine or purpose, and was eventually dispersed through numerous minor battles with authorities and other groups. Master Jacob himself was killed in a skirmish. Yet both the Children's Crusade and the Shepherds' Crusade illustrate how Crusades had filtered down through the feudal layers of Frankish society, and how crusading ideology could easily be taken up by anyone with a spiritual vision and some powers of oratory.

THE ALBIGENSIAN CRUSADE

In France, the notion of the Crusade came to be applicable not only to the struggle against external Islam, but also the internal war on heresy. In essence, the sack of Constantinople at the end of the Fourth Crusade leaned on the notion that the Byzantines' Orthodox faith was, at some level, a heretical deviation from the true path of Latin Christianity. Indeed, during the twelfth century, the concept of a Crusade was broadened out in terms of its theological extent. Now any ostensibly heretical group, regardless of their location or ethnicity, could be the worthy objective of a Crusade. Some argued that it was actually more important to stamp out internal heretics than foreign enemies, because the former poisoned Christ's Church from within.

Below: Innocent III proclaims the Albigensian Crusade in 1209. The Pope felt that the Cathars' lack of respect for offical Church theology and ministers could not be tolerated.

CATHARISM

CATHARISM WAS A DUALISTIC religion, positing existence as an eternal struggle between good and evil, the latter embodied in the physical world (or *Rex Mundi,* 'King of the World') and the former in the pure spirit of the divine. Consequently, the true exponents of Catharism, known as *Perfecti* (the Perfects), rejected the temptations of the material world, living lives with ascetic self-discipline. *Perfecti* were distinguished from ordinary members, *credentes* (Believers), by having undergone a special ceremony called a *consolamentum* – a form of baptism but with the laying on of hands instead of the anointing with or immersion in water. Practices such as sexual chastity and vegetarianism alone set the Cathars apart from the rest of society, but what marked them for the papacy was their rejection of the Catholic priesthood as the centre of spiritual authority, plus their belief that ordinances such as baptism, communion and confession were not the preserve of the Church, but could be practised by ordinary people, albeit with their own distinctive takes on the rites.

Above: In a legendary dispute between St Dominic and the Cathars, holy books were thrown onto a fire, but only Dominic's survived the flames.

The landmark Crusade against heretics was the Albigensian Crusade, which convulsed southern France for two insidious decades (1209–29). The focus of the Crusade was the practitioners of an esoteric form of Christianity known as Catharism, or Albigensianism, after the city of Albi in the

Languedoc province of southern France, where the faith was particularly well established. Catharism was not a large movement by any means; at its height, there were probably about 4000 *perfecti* (the Perfects). Yet it attracted the suspicions of the Church and the French state. Catholic missions to convert the Cathars had failed, plus the Cathars had much support and many practitioners within the nobility, who respected the movement for its evident self-discipline and its apparent transcendence over the corruption and failings that plagued the Catholic Church. That the Cathars held an unflattering mirror up to the Latin Church was another reason for the growth of papal enmity.

THAT THE CATHARS HELD AN UNFLATTERING MIRROR UP TO THE LATIN CHURCH WAS ANOTHER REASON FOR THE GROWTH OF PAPAL ENMITY.

The Cathars grew increasingly more powerful in their region, particularly under the umbrella of one Count Raymond VI of Toulouse. In January 1208, Pope Innocent III sent a legate, Peter of Castelnau, to open discussions with Raymond, but when Peter was murdered the gloves came off. In March, Pope Innocent officially called for a Crusade against the Cathars.

As with any Crusade, the Pope offered indulgences for all who took the cross. Although King Philip Augustus was not a participant, he reluctantly authorized the campaign. There were plenty of aggrieved, bored or cruelly pious nobles who sensed a brutal adventure. Leading figures among them included Simon IV de Montfort and the Counts of Blois and Champagne.

Some 10,000 crusaders had gathered in Lyon by mid 1209. When they launched the Crusade, so began an awful period in French history, characterized by the depressingly regular acts of bestial inhumanity. One of the many low points was the brief siege of Béziers in July 1209, the operation commanded in person by the papal legate Arnaud Amalric. When the city finally fell, it is reputed that Amalric said: 'Kill them all! God will know his own.' Whether he actually said this or not is questionable, but what is not is that some 15,000 people were massacred, despite the fact that only about 700 are estimated to have been Cathars.

Opposite: A massacre of 'heretics' during the Albigensian Crusade in 1211. The number of citizens killed is estimated at more than 200,000 during the lifespan of the Crusade.

Béziers takes its place amongst a litany of crimes. The Albigensian Crusade was not entirely a one-sided affair, however, as more power players were sucked into the conflict, such as Peter II of Aragon, who at one point even fought open battles against Simon de Montfort in 1213. Nevertheless, the forces that gathered against the Cathars, including those of Louis VIII and Louis IX, ultimately crushed their opponents, and Raymond VII, the son of Raymond VI, accepted a peace settlement in 1229, one in which his lands would eventually pass to the rival northern House of Capet on his death. By 1330, Cathars had disappeared from the spiritual map of France.

THE CRUSADES IN THE FAR NORTH

The medieval pagan peoples who clustered around the southern and eastern shores of the Baltic Sea were of multiple ethnicities, world views and cultures. There was no regional unity; wars between the pagan states were common, and would later provide cracks that the crusaders would widen to their advantage. Yet although the Baltic states did not rival the Christian powers individually (with the possible exception of Lithuania), the Christian world was nevertheless fearful of potential pagan expansionism. The pagan tribes were individually on a relatively small scale, but through alliances and connections their power could be increased. Lithuania, for example, had formed a state of significant scale and authority by the beginning of the thirteenth century. The pagans of Prussia, furthermore, were spreading south and west, raiding across the borders of Pomerania and Poland. Combined with wider threats to Christendom from Vikings, Muslims and, potentially, Orthodox Christianity, Catholic Europe was feeling beleaguered and eager to protect its frontiers through active campaigning.

Many states, particularly those of the Holy Roman Empire, found the Baltic region highly attractive for the commercial opportunities it offered, being rich in raw materials such as timber, fur, grain and wax, and with excellent fishing. In the early 1140s, Count Adolf II of Holstein pursued a Christianization of the east Slavic lands, in the process developing Lübeck as a major

Opposite: The sack of Béziers in 1209; a painting by Jean-Noel Sylvestre. The inhabitants of the town make a futile attempt to prevent the entry into the city of the soldiers of the French army, commanded by Arnaud Amalric.

port on the Baltic Sea. Yet the notion of a Crusade against the pagan people of northern Europe really took shape as an annex to the declaration of the Second Crusade in 1147. (In fact, in 1108 a Flemish cleric even implored German intervention against the pagan threat, asking for a campaign similar to that of the First Crusade to Jerusalem.) On 13 April, Pope Eugenius had issued a papal bull intended mainly to assign a crusading role to the German Saxons, who preferred to take their crusading energies north against the pagan peoples of what are today the Baltic states, rather than journey south and east to the Holy Land. Crucially, the Pope decreed that the spiritual rewards for combating the pagans would be the same as those for campaigning against the Muslims.

YET THE NOTION OF A CRUSADE AGAINST THE PAGAN PEOPLE OF NORTHERN EUROPE REALLY TOOK SHAPE AS AN ANNEX TO THE DECLARATION OF THE SECOND CRUSADE IN 1147.

The consequence was the Wendish Crusade, in which the Germans invaded the lands of the Slavic tribes known as 'Wends', pagan peoples who lived in a territory that is today north-east Germany and Poland. Incursions into Wendish lands actually began in 1140, but in 1147, an ill-advised Wendish pre-emptive raid by pagan chief Niklot brought a three-front invasion by Germans, Poles and Danes. Despite facing combined threats from multiple directions, the Wends nevertheless managed to put up an admirable resistance, putting the crusading armies into retreat, disarray and infighting. But, over time, the periodic return of crusading armies, plus the inevitable trade and cultural accommodations with neighbouring Christians, wore down the Wendish identity and unity. In 1185 the last flicker of effective resistance went out with the defeat of the Wendish prince Bogislav by the Danes.

The theme of an anti-pagan Crusade was maintained throughout the twelfth century. In 1171 or 1172, for example, Pope Alexander III issued the papal bull entitled *Non parum animus noster*, in which he declared, to the Christian rulers of Scandinavia, that Crusades should be launched against the pagan Finns and Estonians. The opening of the bull ran as follows:

We are highly distressed and greatly worried to hear of savage Estonians and other pagans in these regions, who rise against and fight God's faithful and against those who labour for the Christian faith and defend the virtue of the Christian name. [You should] gird yourselves, armed with celestial weapons and the strength of Apostolic exhortations, to defend the truth of the Christian faith bravely and to expand the Christian faith forcefully.

One important point about the Northern Crusades is that in addition to military campaigning – the Popes made it quite clear that killing pagans was an acceptable pursuit – the crusaders would also make attempts at conversion. A proselytizing outlook was not really a factor of the Crusades to the Holy Land, despite the fact that both Christianity and Islam stemmed from the same monotheistic root.

Crusades of the Teutonic Knights

One group of individuals who took a central prominence in the Northern Crusades, and indeed built considerable power on the back of their conquests, was the Teutonic Knights. Also known as the Teutonic Order, the Teutonic Knights were another example of highly muscular Christianity, with warrior monks essentially acting as elite mercenaries to prosecute the Crusades. The game-changing campaign for the Teutonic Knights was the Prussian Crusade. This Baltic operation began in 1217, when Pope Honorius III sent a papal bull to bishop Christian of Oliva in March 1217,

Below: A dramatic combat scene from the Prussian Crusade, with Teutonic Knights battling the pagan forces c. 1217. Fighting in Prussia would go on until 1274.

THE TEUTONIC KNIGHTS

Right: Grand Master Hermann von Salza was a skilled diplomat who forged deeper bonds between the Teutonic Knights and the papacy.

ALONGSIDE THE HOSPITALLERS AND the Knights Templar, the Teutonic Knights were one of the greatest of the Military Orders during the age of the Crusades. The foundations of the Teutonic Knights were laid in 1189/90, when a group of German merchants established a hospital in Acre, which was under siege, called the Hospital of St Mary of the German House in Jerusalem. The organization received papal approval, and in 1198 it was decreed a Military Order, in the process granted large areas of land in the Kingdom of Jerusalem and Germany, the Order holding the lands as papal fiefdoms.

The Teutonic Knights were now, in essence, a body of religious mercenaries. Their military skills were undoubted; they were justifiably reputed as some of the finest and most skilled warriors in Christendom. Like the Hospitallers and Templars, furthermore, they accreted considerable power and landholdings. During the thirteenth century, especially under the leadership of the grand master Hermann von Salza (r. 1210–39), the Order of the Teutonic Knights repositioned itself in Europe rather than the Holy Land. In 1211, it went to Hungary to aid King Andrew protect the Hungarian borders against the Cumans, although the Order was eventually expelled in 1225 owing to its growing power and political demands. From Hungary the Knights then went to Poland, to assist Conrad of Masovia with campaigns against the Prussians. As part of this arrangement, Frederick II, the Holy Roman Emperor, issued a bull that gave the Order all of the lands that they could conquer from the Prussians. The Pope then decreed that such lands conquered would

be the property of the Holy See, although given to the Order in perpetual tenure; later a third of the land taken would be assigned back to Church use.

The Order's involvement in the thirteenth-century Prussian and Livonian Crusades, plus other campaigns, created a major landmass in Northern Europe directly under control of the Teutonic Knights, from its headquarters in Marienburg. Its power extended over Prussia, East Pomerania, Livonia, Estonia and large parts of Germany. As with many of the Military Orders, however, the very strength of the Teutonic Knights gradually brought with it suspicion and opposition, particularly from Poland and Lithuania. Military defeats and financial decline in the fifteenth century gradually set the Order on an unstoppable decline. By the early sixteenth century, it was a shadow of its former self, and had utterly disappeared by the beginning of the nineteenth century.

Below: The Teutonic fortress of Marienburg, located near the town of Malbork, Poland. It constitutes the world's largest brick castle and is today a UNESCO World Heritage site.

Above: The Treaty of Meaux-Paris, ratified by Raymond VII, Count of Toulouse and Louis IX of France on 12 April 1229, ended the Albigensian Crusade, with Raymond acknowledging his defeat.

allowing him, with Danish and Polish support, to begin prosecuting a Crusade against the pagan Prussians, who had been a restive presence in north-eastern Europe for more than two centuries.

Polish efforts to subdue the Prussians had been largely unsuccessful, so in 1230 the Teutonic Knights brought their own brand of professionalism and spirit to the Crusade. After a long and winding campaign, plus several major uprisings against Teutonic authority, the Knights finally managed to establish their dominance and rule over Prussia, and subsequently turned it into one of the most successful of the Northern Christian states.

The Teutonic Knights would also come to have a controlling influence over the land of Livonia, a territory that today roughly incorporates Latvia and Estonia. The 'Livonian Crusade' is another of those simplifying historical blanket terms, describing a wearying conflict that rumbled on through most of the thirteenth century. Christian campaigns against Livonia began in 1198, following earlier fruitless attempts at conversion strategies. One of the first military actions, led by Bishop Berthold of Hanover, was roughly quashed by the Livonians – Berthold was killed – in response to which Pope Innocent III issued a bull calling for a Crusade against the Livonians.

In 1202, to assist in the suppression of the Livonian resistance, the Order of the Brothers of the Sword was formed by the third Bishop of Livonia, Albert von Buxhoevden, and consecrated by the Pope in 1204. While they were meant to reflect the best values of the Military Orders, in reality they became known for their criminal levels of violence and inhumanity, which earned them reprimands from the Pope.

The campaigns, however, went well enough for Livonia to be renamed Terra Mariana on 2 February 1207, a principality of the Holy Roman Empire, although in 1215 Pope Innocent III declared the territory under papal authority. In 1237, following the Brothers' massive defeat by the Livonians at the battle of Saule, the Order was made a branch of the Teutonic Knights. Together, the two Orders managed to suppress the Livonian

THE BATTLE ON THE ICE, 1242

A BATTLE OF HISTORICAL note amongst the many fought during the Northern Crusades was the Battle on the Ice, also known as the Battle of Lake Peipus, on 5 April 1242. The combatants were, on one side, the Republic of Novgorod, an east slavic state occupying extensive territory in what is today northern Russia, led by Prince Alexander Nevsky, and the forces of the Livonian Order and the Bishopric of Dorpat, led by Bishop Hermann of Dorpat. The Teutonic Knights began campaigning against Novgorod in September 1240, capturing Pskov, Izborsk, and Koporye, although Nevsky reclaimed Pskov and Koporye the subsequent year. The ongoing clashes between the Novgorodians and the Order built up to the clash on Lake Peipus, which at this time of year was still frozen hard. Alexander deliberately drew his forces up on the shoreline, knowing that it would compel the enemy to cross the ice, problematic for foot soldiers but especially for the hooves of the cavalry. As he predicted, the Teutonic Knights launched a determined and spirited cavalry charge, one that threatened to buckle the Russian infantry lines, but which also exhausted knights and mounts in the execution. At the right moment, Alexander then released his flanking forces, including his cavalry, and the Knights were soon surrounded, and forced into a painful retreat, suffering heavy casualties from cavalry sword and spear and archery fire. Although not a large battle in the scheme of the Northern Crusades, the engagement marked the limit of the Teutonic Knights' advance east.

resistance over time, and Livonia eventually became thoroughly Christianized. The region was governed by the Teutonic Knights as a Livonian Confederation, a mixture of ecclesiastical, free and Teutonic-administered territories.

Another major crusading campaign for the Teutonic Knights, plus the Livonian Order (an autonomous branch of the Teutonic Knights, formed in 1237), was Lithuania. As noted above, Lithuania had some muscle, particularly by the time the Orders began fighting there in earnest from 1283. The well-organized military defences of Lithuania, aided by some wild and barren

Above: The classic vision of the Teutonic Knight. The surcoat with the black cross was adopted by the Knights in 1205.

land on its borders, meant that the Orders achieved little but raiding over the next century. In 1386, the Grand Duchy converted to Christianity, but the Teutonic Knights viewed the conversion sceptically, and continued their military campaigning.

Lithuania finally extinguished the Order of the Teutonic Knight's aspirations for their lands at the battle of Grunwald, fought on 15 July 1410. This vast engagement was a clash of more than 20,000 Teutonic Knights (commanded by Grand Master Ulrich von Jungingen) and their allies against an army of up to 39,000 men of the Kingdom of Poland (King Wladyslaw II Jagiello) and the Grand Duchy of Lithuania (Grand Duke Vytautas). At Grunwald the Order suffered a calamitous defeat; a final desperate charge by the Knights' cavalry reserve resulted

in von Jungingen's death and the crusading army's collapse and dispersal. They subsequently managed a successful defence of Marienburg, but a peace agreement, signed in 1411, had a severe financial impact on the Order, and it never recovered its losses.

The Northern Crusades brought much turmoil and bloodshed to Northern Europe. Unlike the campaigns in the Middle East, the crusaders in the northern climes did not have a focal point equivalent to Jerusalem in the Holy Land. Instead, territorial acquisition was the main objective, allied to the spiritual goals of conversion or extermination of the pagan peoples – either was acceptable. The Northern Crusades are therefore another example of how malleable the crusading ideal could be, modified to suit specific, regional ambitions.

Below: The battle of Grunwald on 15 July 1240 was disastrous for the Teutonic Order; about 80 per cent of the Teutonic Knights who participated were killed.

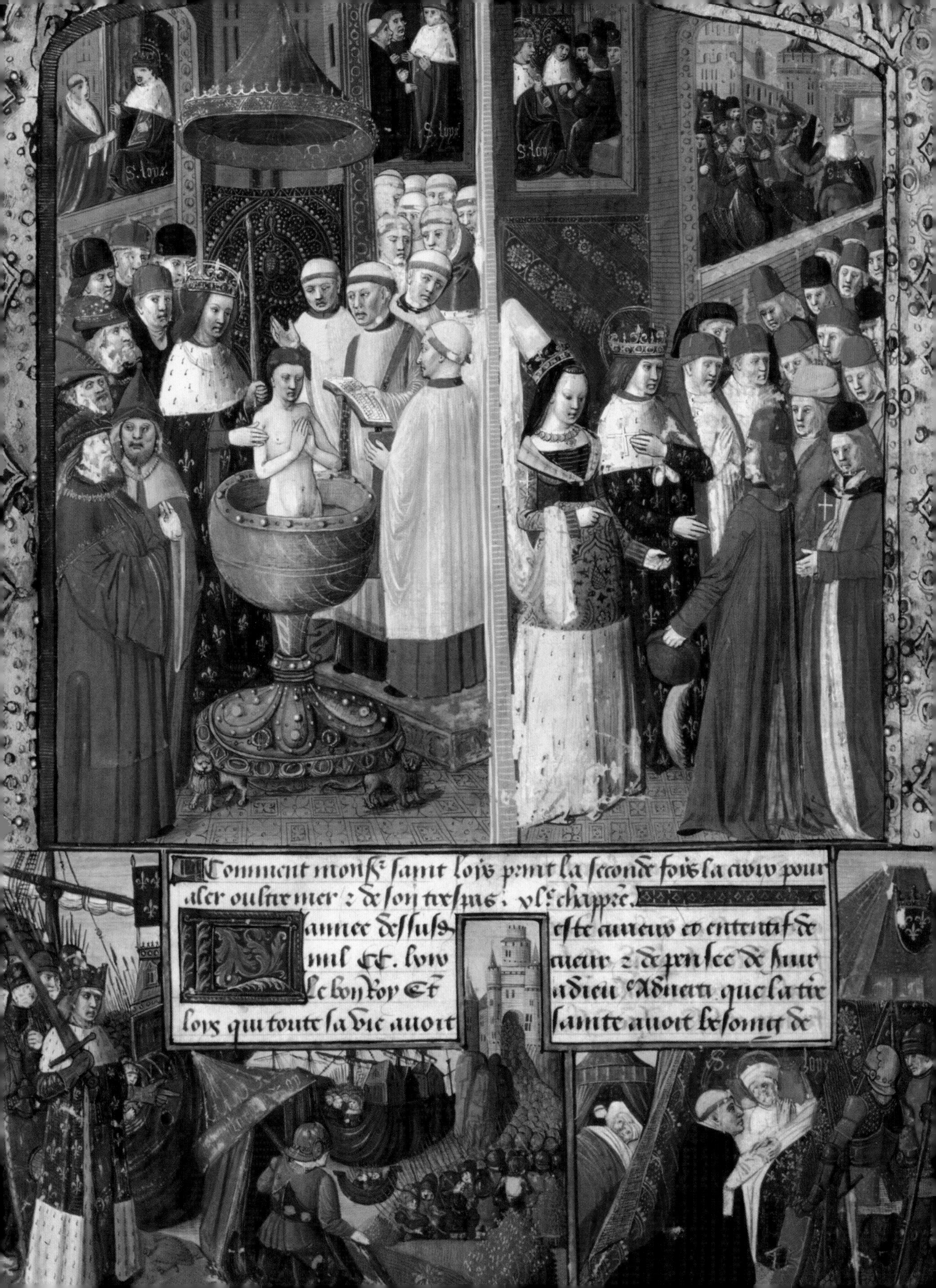
S. loys
S. loys
S. loys
Comment mons. saint lois print la seconde fois la croix pour
aler oultre mer. & de son trespas. vl.e chappre.
Lannee dessus
mil CC. lxx
le bon roy St
lois qui toute sa vie avoit
este ardant et ententif de
cuer & de pensee de servir
a dieu. Advint que la ter
sainte avoit besoing de

7

THE LAST OF THE CRUSADES

The first four Crusades, as we have seen, had the rise-and-fall trajectory common to many great religious and imperial ambitions of this age. From its highpoint at the end of the First Crusade, each subsequent Crusade seemed to dig deeper into either defeat or ambiguous outcomes. The subsequent centuries progressively closed the lid on the crusading spirit, as the Holy Land receded ever further from European influence.

FOR MUCH of the first two decades of the thirteenth century, prevailing truces between Muslims and Christians in the Holy Land had bought some measure of status quo. In July 1210, a long-standing truce between Outremer and the Ayyubid Sultan of Egypt and Syria, al-Adil, expired, but was renewed for five years shortly thereafter by John of Brienne in September 1210. (John was the titular King of Jerusalem following his marriage to Maria, Queen of Jerusalem.) Apparently, John had little appetite for an indefinite accommodation with the Muslims, however, and sent messages to Pope Innocent III requesting that a new Crusade be prepared to recover the Holy Land.

Opposite: Scenes from the life of St Louis (Louis IX of France): his departure on Crusade with Marguerite of Provence; the baptism of a Jew in his presence; the French landing at Carthage in 1270; and finally, his death from dysentery in the same year.

Pope Innocent needed little encouragement to consider a fresh Crusade. Indeed, he was generally preoccupied by such thoughts, feeling that a new campaign would tie in nicely with Christian eschatological predictions for the return of Christ. Planning for the Crusade began in earnest in 1213, but it was publicly defined and declared at the Fourth Lateran Council in 1215.

THE FIFTH CRUSADE

Subsequently, preachers were sent out, carrying the message to all corners of European Christendom, but it soon became apparent that they had a hard sell – both the public and many of Europe's rulers had grown a little weary of the Holy Land Crusade, for understandable historical reasons. Pope Innocent, appearing to recognize the inertia that might face his recruitment policy, included some canny provisions to swell his numbers.

Below: Pope Innocent III preaches for the recovery of the Holy Land – what would become the Fifth Crusade – at the Fourth Lateran Council, held in Rome in late 1215.

For example, a noble or knight could appoint someone in his place to attend the Crusade – a crusader by proxy, if you will – but the sponsor would nevertheless accrue all the spiritual benefits as those who attended in person. By such means, and lots of other encouragements, an army was raised, headed by King Andrew II of Hungary (although his authority later clashed with that of John of Brienne); his forces were subsequently bolstered by manpower brought by Duke Leopold VI of Austria and King Hugh of Cyprus.

Left: Honorius III was Pope Innocent III's successor in 1216. He died in 1277, with Jerusalem still in Muslim hands.

One figure conspicuously missing from this force was Frederick II of Germany, who at the time of Innocent's call for the Crusade was King of Sicily, Germany and Italy; he would become the Holy Roman Emperor in 1220. Frederick had the capacity to bring enormous military and financial resources to the table, and in 1215 he also publicly took the cross. Nevertheless, for complex strategic reasons the papacy initially relieved him of commitment to the forthcoming Crusade. He doesn't appear to have been particularly enthusiastic about it anyway, but raised eyebrows at his absence would eventually compel him to take more direct action.

PREACHERS WERE SENT OUT, CARRYING THE MESSAGE TO ALL CORNERS OF EUROPEAN CHRISTENDOM, BUT IT SOON BECAME APPARENT THAT THEY HAD A HARD SELL.

The Fifth Crusade, to describe it with conventional historical terminology, faced many practical hurdles in its launch, not least issues with sourcing adequate shipping. But eventually it arrived in Acre, that now rather isolated crusader outpost, in September 1217. By this time, Pope Innocent had died (there were rumours of his poisoning) and had been replaced by Pope

FREDERICK II'S DARK INTERESTS

FREDERICK II WAS A formidable individual personally; a true warrior (he was especially skilled with the sword and the bow), athletic and domineering. He was a medieval dualist in nature: he possessed the familiar capacity for cruelty, but was also intellectual and cultured (he could speak German, French and Latin). He had an intense affection for exotic wildlife and also the art of falconry; his treatise *De Arte Venandi cum Avibus (The Art of Hunting with Birds)*, written in the 1240s, remains a highly-regarded source for falconry, as much for its practical investigations as its scholarly insights.

Above: Frederick II was a keen ornithologist, especially authoritative when it came to birds of prey and falconry.

Frederick's intellectual interests were indeed broad. He was especially absorbed by mathematics and philosophy, subjects that gave him familiarity with many Greek and Arabic thinkers; this knowledge opened a cultural insight useful in his future diplomatic negotiations with the Muslim world. Yet there was a darker side to Frederick's inquisitive investigations, made possible by naked power. He conducted experiments in language deprivation, raising some young orphans in isolation from human verbal interaction, to see if over time they would express themselves naturally in a sacred, innate language (they didn't), even though Frederick himself was not particularly fervent in his Christian faith. Even more unpleasantly, the chronicler monk Salimbene di Adam recorded that Frederick conducted mortal experiments, such as consigning someone to die inside a barrel, to see if their soul would escape from a small hole drilled in the woodwork, and of disembowelling people to compare rates of digestion. At the same time, Frederick was also a genuine patron of more conventional intellectual development; he founded the University of Naples in 1224. It appears to have been this mix of black cruelty and a sharp mind that made Frederick such a forceful presence on the medieval stage.

Honorius III, who took the papacy on 18 July 1216. Honorius was just as much an enthusiast for the Crusade as Innocent; in particular, he was sharply focused on bringing Frederick II on Crusade as soon as feasible, seeing in him the best possibility for overwhelming the Muslims and recovering the Holy Land. For now, however, the chief objective of the crusader leadership was an assault upon Egypt, the centre of the sultanate's power. The crusader army would be bolstered by the addition of local forces from Outremer: those of John of Brienne and the contribution of Prince Bohemund IV, the ruler of Antioch.

The first phase of the Fifth Crusade lasted from November 1217 until February 1218, and expressed itself in a string of minor local victories for the crusaders. Sultan al-Adil's army was defeated by the Christians at the battle of Bethsaida on 10 November, and the Muslim forces faced further assaults on some of their fortresses in Syria and Lebanon. Al-Adil was certainly rattled by the crusader aggression, but the crusading army started to fritter its opportunities, particularly as Andrew II became satisfied with the haul of loot he had already won. He was also suffering from illness, and so with weakened resolve he left the Crusade in January 1218, taking many of the crusaders with him.

Below: A combat scene from the Fifth Crusade. The axes seen were particularly useful for smashing open plate armour.

Here was not the end of the Fifth Crusade, however. In the springtime, reinforcements from Germany arrived, under the direction of Oliver of Cologne, plus other troops of Dutch, Flemish and Frisian descent commanded by Count William I of Holland. It was this army, under the overall command of John of Brienne, that set out from Acre in May 1218, bound for Egypt. As they did so, Keykavus I, Seljuk Sultan of Rum in Anatolia, also began a campaign against Ayyubid Syria; taking advantage of fractured Muslim relations, the Christians had made an alliance with the Seljuks.

The main objective of the Egyptian campaign was the strategically well-placed port city of Damietta, where the crusaders arrived on 29 May. A lengthy siege began, one that would inflict heavy attrition on both sides. The first phase of the siege was devoted to capturing a sizeable guard tower, used as an anchor point for a defensive chain that stretched across the harbour entrance. This alone was not achieved until late August; it can't have been encouraging that the city itself boasted 28 defensive towers. A morale-boosting moment, however, came with news of the death of al-Adil on 31 August; he was succeeded by Sultan al-Kamil.

Above: This fifteenth century illuminated manuscript shows the papal legate, Pelagius, waiting to disembark at Damietta, as troops prepare to besiege the city in 1218.

Disease and serious hunger started to run through the crusader camp as the siege stretched on through the year. There were also problems at the top. Keen to stamp papal authority over the Crusade, Pope Honorius had sent a force of mainly French crusaders under Cardinal Pelagius, Bishop of Albano and Legate of the Apostolic See, who upon his arrival began to wrestle with John of Brienne over strategy, claiming the supremacy of Church authority.

The consequences of this command dissent were to be profound. In February 1219, the weakened al-Kamil raised the prospect of a truce. His proposal seemed to contain the golden ticket – he offered to return the Kingdom of Jerusalem, including Jerusalem, Bethlehem and Nazareth, to the crusaders, along with the True Cross. John of Brienne, and many of the nobles, were naturally eager to accept this offer, but Pelagius belligerently rejected it – he would not countenance negotiations with the Muslims. Thus the siege of Damietta rolled on until the city was finally taken, virtually unguarded, on 5 November 1219.

The Crusade now hit something of a hiatus, the crusaders deeply wearied by the siege experience. In July 1221, however, Pelagius, keen to regain momentum, led out a force accompanied by a reluctant John of Brienne, heading for Cairo. En route, the army stopped to make camp by the River Nile, which unbeknown to Pelagius was susceptible to flooding at this time of year. The Egyptians, utterly familiar with the natural rhythms of their own land, used the rising water levels to manoeuvre their ships to cut off the Christian supply fleet, then they opened sluice gates that poured acres of river water across the landscape occupied by the crusaders. Thrown into disarray and logistical collapse, the crusaders were compelled to retreat by 8 September. To add to their humiliation, given that they had rejected a diplomatic opportunity to take back the Holy Land, Pelagius was compelled to sign an eight-year truce with al-Kamil, accompanied by the evacuation of Damietta.

Below: Frederick II rides into Jerusalem in 1229. He actually passed through the streets in almost total silence, the locals expressing no joy at his arrival.

THE SIXTH CRUSADE

The Sixth Crusade of 1228–29 is the moment when Frederick II steps fully into the spotlight, finally taking an active role in the Crusades. Frederick had by this time been crowned Holy Roman Emperor, and his marriage to Empress Isabella II of Jerusalem, the daughter of John of Brienne, in November 1225, meant that Frederick could claim the title King of Jerusalem. This all meant that Frederick was invested in the future of the Holy Land, but the papacy was increasingly frustrated by Frederick's apparent lack of willingness to make an actual campaign. During a meeting with papal officials in July 1225, Frederick had even been placed under the harshest of deadlines – if he did not lead a Crusade to the east by August 1227 he would be excommunicated. Frederick did eventually mobilize his forces, in September 1227, but a subsequent illness delayed his campaign even further. By this time, a new Pope was in office – the unwavering Gregory IX – and he followed through on the excommunication. His was not a popular decision with many. In one instance, during an Easter service in Rome in 1228, Gregory was forced to flee the cathedral when, after renewing the excommunication, the gathered congregation rioted in support of the German Emperor.

FREDERICK HAD EVEN BEEN PLACED UNDER THE HARSHEST OF DEADLINES – IF HE DID NOT LEAD A CRUSADE TO THE EAST BY AUGUST 1227 HE WOULD BE EXCOMMUNICATED.

Despite his apparent alienation from the Church, Frederick nevertheless committed himself to the Crusade in 1228, departing from Brindisi with 4000 troops on 28 June. It was an army imbued with professionalism and discipline, unified under their capable leader. What Frederick did not possess, however, was the unquestioning support of Christians in the Holy Land. He was seen as something of an interloper, not helped by his excommunication – a fact that particularly strained relations with the Church-centric Templars and Hospitallers. Also, the previous May, Isabella had died in childbirth. Frederick now took the regency for the surviving infant king, Conrad, much to the chagrin of John of Brienne, who felt this outsider muscling in on his power. The stress fractures that were already showing in crusader relations would widen considerably over the coming months.

Nevertheless, Frederick began his land campaign in early 1229, marching out from Acre towards Jaffa. News of his excommunication had reduced Frederick's recruiting potential significantly, but he had the advantage of an enemy in disarray. Al-Kamil was facing numerous threats from within the Muslim world. Worst of all, his own brother al-Muazzam, ruler of Damascus, had made an alliance with Khwarazmian Turks against al-Kamil in northern Iraq; al-Muazzam died in 1227, but his son, al-Nasir Dawud, took up the mantle of hostility to his uncle.

Both Frederick and al-Kamil recognized their positions of weakness, and the result was that they came to the negotiating table rather than the field of battle. Frederick would have been aware of al-Kamil's previous offer to bargain away the Holy Land, but the Emperor was also likely inspired to talk by his studied admiration for Arabic culture.

On 18 February 1229, Frederick and al-Kamil signed themselves up to the Peace of Jaffa. Considering that Frederick was acting entirely outside papal authority, it was a remarkable treaty. Key parts of the Holy Land – including Nazareth, Bethlehem and Jerusalem itself – would be returned to Christian control, the Muslims retaining the Temple area. In return, Frederick committed himself to a 10-year truce, including a pledge to defend al-Kamil from his enemies.

Frederick marched into Jerusalem on 17 March 1229. If he had imagined receiving a victorious and triumphant reception, he would be disappointed. Many of the local nobles were angered by their absence from the inter-faith negotiations, plus the local Patriarch had even threatened a blanket excommunication of the city's Christians if they welcomed the errant crusader. Having wandered through resentfully empty streets, on 18 March Frederick literally crowned himself (there was no bishop to officiate) at the Church of the Holy Sepulchre.

Above: Frederick II literally crowns himself King of Jerusalem on 18 March 1229. The Latin Patriarch of the city, Gerald of Lausanne, did not attend the event.

Given that the treaty was floating in such unpromising waters (many Muslim leaders were also opposed to the treaty), its future was always unstable. There were also strategic issues at play. The strip of land returned to the Christians by the treaty was thin, with a long and highly vulnerable flank. Civil conflict erupted in both Jerusalem and in Cyprus (where Frederick claimed suzerainty), as barons rebelled against Frederick's authority. Frederick returned to Europe and made peace with the Pope at San Germano on 23 July 1230; Gregory had actually previously supported an invasion of Sicily, Frederick's domain, by an army under John of Brienne, but Frederick's defeat of this force had helped bring the two men to a rapprochement.

THE ARMIES OF THE KINGDOM OF JERUSALEM WERE VIRTUALLY WIPED OUT BY A COMBINED AYYUBID AND KHWARAZMIAN FORCE AT LA FORBIE.

As for the Holy Land, the divisions and hostilities unleashed by the Sixth Crusade led to disarray and disunity on both sides. In 1239, as the 10-year truce ended, the warring Khwarazmian Muslims retook Jerusalem with little effort, although in 1239–41 Count Thibauld of Champagne and Earl Richard of Cornwall (the brother of Henry III of England) led further Crusades into the Levant, and once again negotiated a treaty for the return of Jerusalem, this time with Sultan al-Salih. But stable relations were not destined to be, and on 17–18 October 1244 the armies of the Kingdom of Jerusalem were virtually wiped out by a combined Ayyubid and Khwarazmian force at La Forbie, northeast of Gaza – 5000 crusaders died and many of the leaders were led off to

Below: In this medieval representation of the battle of La Forbie, crusader cavalry are routed and, to the left, Christians are herded off into captivity.

captivity. Following the battle of La Forbie, which can be viewed as the terminal defeat of Christian Outremer, Jerusalem was once again taken by the Muslims, and was never to be returned.

Below: Louis IX was crowned in Reims at the age of 12, following the death of his father Louis VIII the Lion, although his mother, Blanche of Castile, ruled the kingdom until he reached maturity.

LOUIS IX – THE SEVENTH AND EIGHTH CRUSADES

Although genuine piety has not been absent from our narrative so far, it has often been balanced against, or indeed cancelled out, by the brutal *realpolitik* of the day. Among the crusader leaders, therefore, it is something of a quest to find individuals who truly embody the crusading ideal. Arguably one who does come close is King Louis IX of France (r. 1226–70), who would lead two Crusades in the mid-thirteenth century, and who would later (1297) be canonized by the Church, not so much for his campaigns – both were failures – but for his high standards of behaviour within them. 'Saint Louis', who had come to the throne in 1226, was everything a crusader was meant to represent – deeply religious, with faith driving his every decision; principled in his public and private life; and brave on the battlefield. Given these traits, it seems almost inevitable that at some point he would take the cross and lead a Crusade to the East. And unlike Frederick before him, Louis regarded Christian morality as his benchmark for action, rather than worldly pragmatism, not that it would lead him to any greater success.

Louis took the cross in 1244, but, as was common, financial and political practicalities delayed the first steps. Eventually, by the summer of 1248 the requisite funds had been raised (mostly through ecclesiastical taxation), spurred on by requests for help by the beleaguered vestiges of Outremer and the renewed calls for a Crusade from Pope Innocent IV, although Louis was well aware that the papacy seemed more interested in using the Crusade as leverage in its continuing struggles with Frederick II. In total, Louis raised an army of around 15,000 men, including 3000 knights. On 25 August, it set out from Aigues-Mortes in

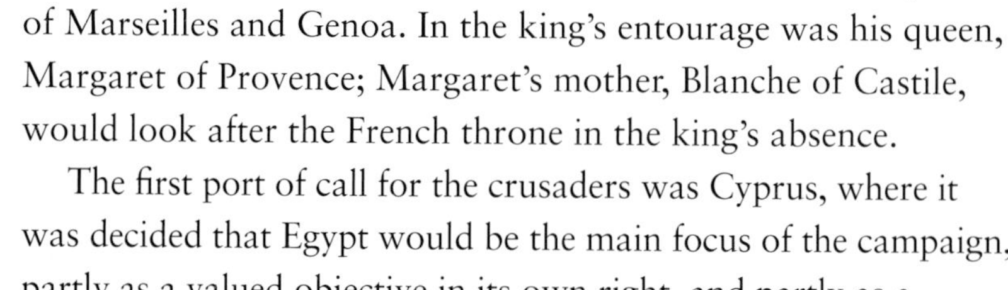

some 300 ships provided under contract by the maritime powers of Marseilles and Genoa. In the king's entourage was his queen, Margaret of Provence; Margaret's mother, Blanche of Castile, would look after the French throne in the king's absence.

The first port of call for the crusaders was Cyprus, where it was decided that Egypt would be the main focus of the campaign, partly as a valued objective in its own right, and partly as a future jumping-off point for direct assaults into the Holy Land. The ruler of Egypt at this time was al-Malik al-Salih, a man who had experienced the cutting-edge of Crusades before – he had been taken hostage during the Fifth Crusade, and had led the capture of Jerusalem following its sacking by the Khwarazmians in 1244. Until the crusaders arrived, al-Malik al-Salih had much on his plate dealing with the wars and power play within the Islamic states. There was also now a new threat to the north – the Mongols, who had swept irresistibly across Eastern and Central Asia and into Eastern Europe, as well as into the Muslim world in the Middle East.

Below: St Louis embarks on the Crusades, his fleet setting sail on their disastrous campaign from Aigues-Mortes, southern France.

The crusader fleet arrived in Cyprus in September 1248, but the onset of winter meant that the campaigning had to be delayed until more clement times the following year. Thus it wasn't until May 1249 that the crusader fleet finally set off from Cyprus, heading towards the same destination as that favoured by Frederick, the port city of Damietta. The army had also received some reinforcements in the meantime, in the form of Franks from Greece; these men added to the small contingent of English troops who were also on the Crusade, giving the army something of an international flavour.

Despite adverse weather delaying and dispersing the crusader fleet during transit, the assault on Damietta began on 5 June.

THE CHARACTER OF LOUIS IX

Above: King Louis I of Navarre, 1309, receiving an account of the life of King Louis IX from its author, Jean de Joinville.

OUR DEFINING PRIMARY SOURCE for gaining insight into Louis IX is the epic *Life of Saint Louis*, written by the French chronicler and lord Jean de Joinville (1224–1317). Joinville not only served within Louis' court but also accompanied him on the Seventh Crusade, becoming one of the king's closest advisors and friends. Here Joinville provides an insight into Louis' personal piety:

The holy man so loved truth that he would not play even the Saracens false, as hereafter you shall hear. Touching his mouth he was sober, for never in my life did I hear him discourse of dishes, as many rich men do; but contentedly he ate whatever his cooks set before him. In words he was temperate, for never did I hear him speak ill of others, nor ever hear him name the Devil; the which is not common throughout the kingdom, and thereat, I bow, God is ill pleased. His wine he tempered moderately, according as he saw that the wine could bear it. He asked me in Cyprus: why I put no water to my wine? and I told him; It was the physicians' doing, who told me, that I had a thick head and a cold belly, and that it was not in me to get drunk. And he said: They deceived me; for unless I used myself whilst young to drink it watered, if, when old, I desired to do so, I should then be seized with gouts and stomach complaints and never have my health: whereas, if in old age I were to take my wine neat, I should be drunk every evening, and that it was a passing foul thing for a gallant gentleman to get drunk. He asked me: Whether I wished to be honoured in this world and win Heaven at my death? 'Yea!' said I, 'Then,' said he, 'See that you be not wittingly guilty of any word or deed whereof if all the world knew it you could not acknowledge: So I said; So I did.'

He bade me avoid contradicting or disagreeing with anything that anyone said before me, provided there would be no blame nor harm to myself in letting it pass; for that hard words provoke quarrels that are the death of thousands.

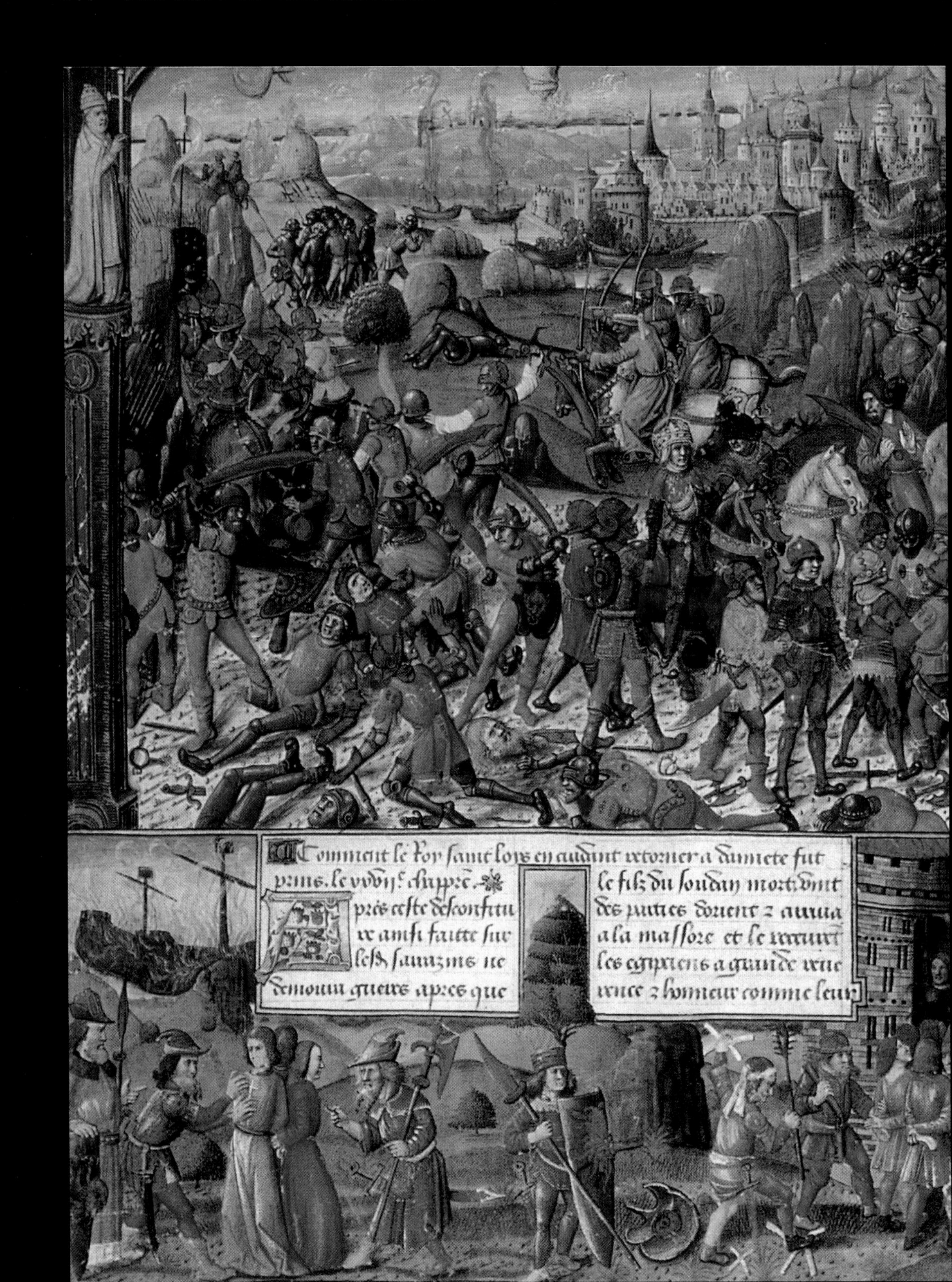
Comment le roy saint loys en cuidant retorner a damiete fut
le filz du soudan mort
a la massore et le

Louis was in the vanguard of the amphibious action, the French troops immediately doing battle with the Muslim troops that had been drawn up on the beaches near the city, in readiness to meet the invaders. By a ferocious determination, the crusaders managed to push the defenders back off the beach and into the city. As the French build-up continued, the garrison of Damietta decided that the city was lost, and thus made an overnight retreat, leaving Louis to lead his army into Damietta without serious contest.

Following discussions, the crusaders decided that the next objective would be Cairo, the centre of Muslim Egyptian power. Al-Malik al-Salih died on 22 November and was succeeded by his son, al-Muazzam Turanshah. To get to Cairo, the crusaders first had to defeat a major Egyptian army in the fortress town of al-Mansurah, across the canal of Ashmum. The spearhead of the crusader force, led by Robert of Artois and accompanied by the English noble William, Earl of Salisbury, moved across the canal in February 1250 and on 8 February attacked a large Muslim camp 3km (2 miles) from al-Mansurah. The Muslim forces here were commanded by men of the Mamluk military caste, a people who had emerged from slave soldiery and who now began an impressive rise to the seats of leadership, altering the balance of power once again in the Muslim world. (The Khwarazmians we encountered above were also of Mamluk descent.) The Muslims, unable to reverse the crusader drive, made a pullback to al-Mansurah, leaving the Christians to occupy their former camp. Then, the Mamluk commander Rukn al-Zahir Baibars carefully laid a trap for the crusaders. He deliberately left the gates of the city open, and when Robert and Williams' men pushed inside the city, they were suddenly ambushed at close quarters. It was a massacre. Both Robert and William were slain, as were most of the warriors with them.

RUKN AL-ZAHIR BAIBARS ... DELIBERATELY LEFT THE GATES OF THE CITY OPEN, AND WHEN ROBERT AND WILLIAMS' MEN PUSHED INSIDE THE CITY, THEY WERE SUDDENLY AMBUSHED.

Meanwhile, the main force of crusaders under Louis had moved up to al-Mansurah, and established a well-fortified

Opposite: King Louis' forces are defeated at the battle of al-Mansurah in 1250. The Muslim forces, very fancifully depicted, place the Christian leaders in chains at the bottom.

camp outside the city. Both sides launched actions against their opponents, but neither seemed to be able to break the stand-off between them. But time was not on Louis' side, and Turanshah knew it – he now attacked the crusaders' logistical chain, intercepting the supply ships running out from Damietta. As the weeks went by, the crusader army thereby sank into the mire of famine, and eventually Louis was compelled to retreat. The retreat itself continued the nightmare, with hundreds dying or collapsing as they walked.

Eventually even Louis was utterly incapacitated by illness, and on 6 April, at the battle of Fariskur, the Muslim forces swamped the stumbling Europeans. Those men who were not killed in battle fell into miserable captivity, including Louis. The prisoners' future was perilous; at one point, to control the numbers, Turanshah ordered that each day for seven days 300 crusaders were to be taken from the mass and executed. The surviving nobles and the king were held for ransom, and only when Damietta was formally ceded to the Muslims and a huge cash ransom paid (Louis' personal ransom was 400,000 dinars), was Louis finally released, on 6 May 1250.

AT ONE POINT, TO CONTROL THE NUMBERS, TURANSHAH ORDERED THAT EACH DAY FOR SEVEN DAYS 300 CRUSADERS WERE TO BE TAKEN FROM THE MASS AND EXECUTED.

JOURNEY TO ACRE

Many expected Louis to return home with grateful speed following his defeat, indeed most actively encouraged him to do so. Yet his strong sense of honour instead compelled him to travel to Acre, to try to bring a positive influence to what was left of Outremer. He stayed there from 1250 to 1254. His presence gave the crusader states a central authority, and indeed Louis worked hard to heal many of the minor fractures and enmities that had blighted Christian unity in Outremer.

What was also critical for Louis was to make the remaining Christian cities properly defendable. Fortress cities such as Acre, Jaffa, Caesarea and Sidon had weakened over the previous turbulent decades, so Louis oversaw the improvement of their physical defences and garrisons. Having completed much valuable

Above: Louis IX's Eighth Crusade, here depicted putting ashore on the Tunisian coast, was quickly decimated by an epidemic of dysentery.

work, Louis finally went home in 1254. He had done enough to secure his reputation as a noble and brave man, but he retained a deep sense of unfinished business.

In the 15 years following Louis' return to France, the religious, political and military landscape of the Middle East and North Africa changed relentlessly. For the Muslims, the greatest threat was that of the Mongol juggernaut. In the late 1250s, Möngke Khan, the Mongol ruler, began campaigning for the conquest of Mesopotamia, Syria and Persia, bringing him, through his warrior brother and commander Hulagu, into direct conflict with the Abbasid caliphate of Baghdad. Once he had subdued Persia, Hulagu took his Mongol army and closed up on Baghdad in late January 1258. After a 13-day siege, the Abbasid resistance collapsed, and the Mongols took Baghdad, unleashing enormous physical destruction and bloodshed – some estimates put the death toll as high as 200,000.

For a time, it seemed that Syria might be the next domino to topple to the Mongols. Then, at the battle of Ayn Jalut, south-

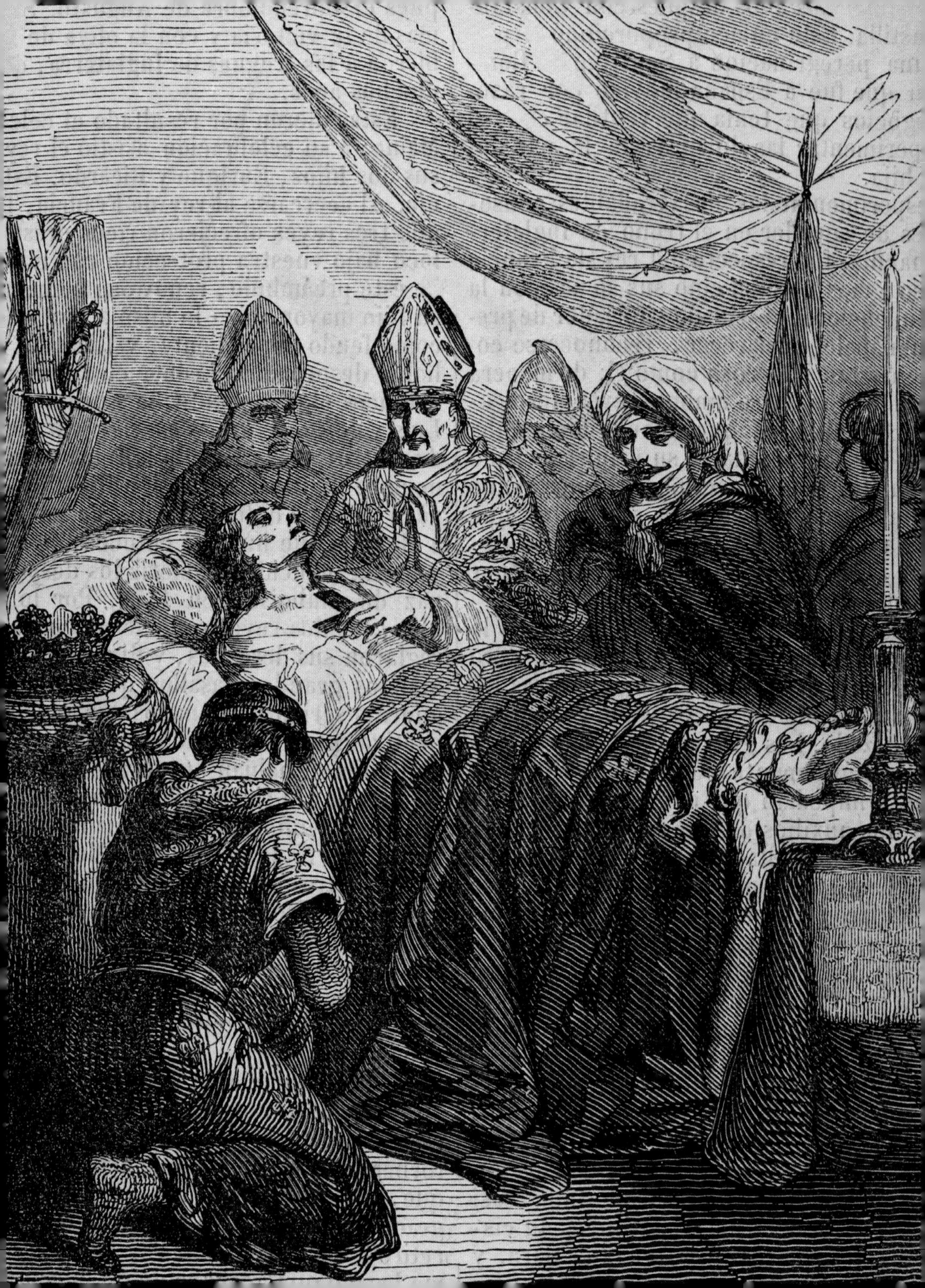

east of Acre, the Malmuks – now the ruling dynasty in Cairo and expanding their power elsewhere – inflicted a heavy defeat on the Mongols that stopped their advance south. It is notable that around this time Bohemund VI of Antioch had tried to read the future winds and had actually formed an alliance with the Mongols, an act that the now-victorious Mamluks would not forget.

In the 1260s, the Mamluks steadily made their move on the Christian outposts of Outremer. Between 1265 and 1268, Caesarea, Haifa, Arsuf, Galilee, Antioch and the fortress of Krac des Chevaliers were all conquered by the armies of Baibars, who had become sultan in 1260. Baibars was a thuggish individual who murdered his way to power. Antioch, once fallen, suffered widespread massacre and destruction that, when reported back to the West, sent shivers throughout European society. King Louis was moved once again to launch a Crusade, feeling it his Christian duty to protect and save those who still remained under the shadow of Islam. In fact, Pope Urban IV had been preaching for a Crusade during the 1260s, specifically with the original objective of taking back Jerusalem for Christendom. Urban's efforts had been largely undone by internal European squabbles and conflicts, but Louis later bought some clarity to the venture.

ANTIOCH SUFFERED WIDESPREAD MASSACRE AND DESTRUCTION THAT, WHEN REPORTED BACK TO THE WEST, SENT SHIVERS THROUGHOUT EUROPEAN SOCIETY.

EIGHTH CRUSADE

King Louis launched what can be classified as the Eighth Crusade on 1 July 1270. Initially, his plan was to sail straight for the Holy Land, via Cyprus. Subsequently, and possibly following consultations with his brother, Charles of Anjou, the plan was changed to make Tunis in North Africa the first staging post. On 1 July, Louis' own fleet sailed from Aigues-Mortes, and the following day another fleet headed by the king of Navarre sailed from Marseille, the two fleets coordinating on the southern coastline of Sicily. From there they proceeded to the North African coast, establishing a camp in the ruins of ancient Carthage.

Opposite: A pious and peaceful artistic representation of the death of Louis IX. His flesh was subsequently boiled away, so that his bones could be transported hygienically back to France.

DISEASE IN THE CRUSADES

AMONGST CRUSADER ARMIES, disease was every bit a killer as battle, in fact often more so, depending on the campaign and conditions. The seminal blights were diseases related to poor sanitation, especially cholera, dysentery (the greatest of all the killers during the twelfth and thirteenth centuries) and typhoid fever, all of which could run like wildfire through the close confines of a camp or a transport ship. There was also a range of viral illnesses that were periodic or persistent in the medieval world – measles, chicken pox, hepatitis and seasonal influenzas are examples (plague came later in medieval history). All the diseases suffered by the crusaders were frequently compounded by poor diet, which lowered the immune response to infections. Sometimes dietary deficiencies could be so pronounced as to result in starvation and scurvy.

Added to these issues were a range of other maladies: malaria, contracted from the clouds of mosquitoes that plagued crusaders around swampland and rivers; leprosy, resulting in horrible skin ulceration and deformities; and intestinal worms that did not typically kill, but brought huge discomfort.

Poor dental hygiene was also a major problem; in fact, dental problems for crusaders were exacerbated by the access to sugary foods in the Levant.

Modern estimates of mortality during the long Crusades are 19–35 per cent among knights and nobles, climbing much higher (possibly to about 50 per cent) for the lower orders. Only about 30 per cent of those who died would be accounted for by combat; disease and malnutrition did the rest. As the Eighth Crusade shows, disease was quite capable of stopping an entire Crusade in its tracks.

But this was as far as the Eighth Crusade got. Chronic disease, especially dysentery, swept through the ranks of the crusaders, killing or incapacitating hundreds. Illness was no respecter of rank, and Louis himself succumbed, and he died on 25 August; his own son, John Tristan, who had accompanied his father on the Crusade, had already died, on 3 August.

The Mamluks and the surviving crusaders came to an accommodation, and the Eighth Crusade faded away in pestilence and disappointment.

THE NINTH CRUSADE

In the 'classical' chronology of the Crusades, the Ninth Crusade is the last major campaign in the narrative, although many historians regard it as more strictly a continuation of the Eighth Crusade. Indeed, the leader of the Ninth Crusade – Prince Edward of England, the future King Edward I (r. 1272–1307) – had originally intended to join Louis IX as he set out on his Crusade in 1270, but was marginally delayed. Thus by the time he did arrive in Tunis, on 10 November, Louis was already dead and the agreement signed with the Muslims prevented Edward from attacking Tunis.

Edward was a warrior by nature, and was frustrated by the apparent impotence forced upon him by earlier events and decisions. His fleet sailed to Sicily, and although some of his English crusaders now decided to head for home, Edward headed east for Acre with about 308 vessels and 1000 troops, including around 200 knights. He arrived there on 9 May 1271, intent on defending what remained of Christian territory against the Mamluk threat from the south and east. Edward was conscious of his numerical inferiority, even when the forces of Outremer were added, thus he attempted to make a military alliance with the Mongols, which was signed on 4 September 1271 with Abagha Khan. The Mongol contribution to Edward's Crusade was significant but not overwhelmingly so; Abagha's involvement in other conflicts meant that he could only send about 10,000 troops, and although these forces made some raids south, eventually they turned back north again with their booty.

Edward's Crusade was rather more a sequence of localized raids, rather than a prolonged campaign aimed at

Below: Edward of England departs for the Holy Land on the Ninth Crusade. His campaign would be largely pointless, and little more than a year after arriving at Acre he was heading for home.

THE MAMLUK ARMY

Above: Cavalry were the strongest element of the Mamluk army, known for their speed and mobility.

THE MAMLUK ARMY WAS one of the most efficient and feared fighting forces of the Middle East during the later centuries of the Crusades. In the field, a Mamluk army tended to consist of three elements. First there were the troops of the royal bodyguard, the sultan's elite and loyal guardians; as part of a regional army, they also acted as guarantor of the sultan's interests, when the force was being led by a regional ruler. Next there were the standard Mamluk regiments of *askari*, and finally there were private units, both those led by senior officers with the bodyguard plus large numbers of mercenaries, typically from Turcoman, Bedouin or Kurdish stock. The Mamluk warriors presented a mixed body of footsoldiers, cavalry and archers. They were generally lightly armoured, or not armoured at all, although the more senior ranks often wore mail hauberks. A well-armed *askari* might carry three weapons into battle: a long javelin, used both as a throwing and as a stabbing weapon; a straight-sided sword or curved sabre for close-quarter fighting; and a short composite bow in a holder on his hip, plus a quiver for about 25–35 arrows.

strategic gain. His army attacked Nazareth first, taking the town with relatively few problems and killing most of the inhabitants, a now almost customary behaviour in an age when life was cheap on both sides. He then made a rather inconsequential raid on St Georges-de-Lebeyne, burning some crops. It was clear that Edward wasn't accomplishing much, but in the autumn of 1271 his brother, Edmund, arrived with much-needed reinforcements, and Edward started to feel more ambitious. His largest action was a raid on the Muslim fortress of Qaqun, 72km (45 miles) from Acre, supported by significant contingents from the Military Orders. There he inflicted about 1500 casualties on a force of Turkoman irregulars, but he did not manage to seize the castle – he likely could not have held it had he done so.

Apart from participating in the successful defence of Acre in December 1271, when the city came under a short siege by Baibars' men, Edward's crusaders did not do much more in physical terms. King Hugh of Jerusalem sealed a treaty with Baibars, signed in May 1272 at Caesarea, that guaranteed the borders of the existing Christian kingdom for 10 years. He also realized that taking Jerusalem was simply not viable, as much on account of Christian divisions as on Muslim strength. Edmund left Acre for home in May.

Edward, mindful of the fragility of peace treaties in this part of the world, stayed on for several more months. During this time, he experienced an assassination attempt on 16 June, when he was attacked in his chambers by a man with a poisoned dagger. Edward survived but received a nasty injury, delaying his departure further. He finally left Acre in September 1172, and following a long circuitous journey arrived home in 1274, where he was crowned King of England in August (his father, Henry III, died during Edward's transit back to England).

KING HUGH OF JERUSALEM SEALED A TREATY WITH BAIBARS, SIGNED IN MAY 1272 AT CAESAREA, THAT GUARANTEED THE BORDERS OF THE EXISTING CHRISTIAN KINGDOM FOR 10 YEARS.

FINAL ACTS

The failure of the Ninth Crusade was, to a large degree, the end of the Crusades in practical terms. Reclaiming the Holy Land, including Jerusalem, was no longer an option or even a possibility. This was not just a case of Muslim supremacy in the region. In the shifting sands of European governance, it became increasingly difficult to gain royal interest in Crusades, especially now that two centuries of precedents hardly gave encouraging signs of likely success. Royal power had grown substantially in relation to papal authority, meaning that it was harder for Popes to gather a Crusade under their centralizing influence. Furthermore, much of Outremer was now governed by rulers who did not actually live there, creating tensions that fostered divisions and conflict. Outremer was not a unified entity, and that terminally weakened it.

Opposite: The Hospitalier marshall Matthieu de Clermont defiantly defends the walls of Acre in 1291 against the Muslim attackers. The city fell after a six-week siege.

In 1282, the 10-year truce between Outremer and the Mamluks came to an end. Efforts to achieve a defensive alliance between the Christians and the Mongols came to nothing, and thus from the late 1280s the Muslim forces moved in for the kill. Tripoli was taken in 1289. Then in 1291, Acre – that most persistent outpost of Christendom – fell after a six-week siege. This was a terrible blow psychologically for the Church, and the absolute nature of the defeat was reinforced by the massacre and enslavement of its peoples. The testimony of the Master of the Hospital in Acre, John de Villiers, sums up the sheer dejection and fear of the helpless population:

> *On that same day I was stricken nearly to death by a lance between my shoulders, a wound that has made writing this letter a very difficult task. Meanwhile, a great crowd of Saracens were entering the city on all sides, by land and by sea, moving along the walls, which were all pierced and broken, until they came to our shelters. Our sergeants, lads and mercenaries, and the crusaders and others, gave up all hope and fled towards the ships, throwing down their arms and armour. We and our brothers, the greatest number of whom were mortally wounded or gravely injured, resisted them as long as we could, God knows. And as some of us were lying as if we were half-dead and lay in a faint before our enemies, our sergeants and our household boys came and carried me, mortally wounded, and our other brothers away, at great danger to themselves.*

This is not the same as saying that the crusading ideal faded away; rather it stayed persistent for more than a century following Edward's departure from Acre, and even lingered on into the fifteenth century. Thus there were a series of crusading campaigns beyond the Ninth Crusade, although none directed into the former lands of Outremer. The first came in 1365, when King Peter I of Cyprus – the titular King of Jerusalem – took 10,000 men and 4000 horses on a crusade to Egypt. This action had one crowning success, the capture of Alexandria, a result that brought huge bounty for Peter (the city was sacked and the population massacred). There was the possibility that taking Alexandria might be the first step towards a campaign into the Holy Land itself – Peter did launch some actions against the ports on the Syrian coast – but European and papal praise did not translate into hard support, and Alexandria was eventually relinquished by treaty in 1370 (Peter had actually been assassinated by this time, killed by three of his own knights on 17 January 1396).

From the mid-fourteenth century, Europe's alarm was mounting over Islamic expansion once again, this time the threat of the Ottoman Turks who had poured into the Balkans, conquering Greece and Bulgaria and threatening Constantinople. In response to this direct threat to Europe, another Crusade was mustered, responding to a request for support from King Sigismund of Hungary. The result was the Crusade of Nicopolis, what some historians have actually termed the Last Crusade. Its name comes for the eponymous battle fought south of the River Danube on 25 September 1396, between on one side the forces of Sigismund and John, Count of Nevers, and on the other the Ottoman Turks led by Sultan Bayezid I. It was a major engagement, with approximately 15,000 crusaders and possibly the same number of Ottomans (including some Serbian allies), but it resulted in a hammering defeat for the crusaders. A potential Ottoman exploitation of the victory westwards was only quashed by Bayezid's defeat at the hands of the great Mongol leader Tamerlane, at the battle of Ankara in July 1402.

EUROPE'S ALARM WAS MOUNTING OVER ISLAMIC EXPANSION ONCE AGAIN, THIS TIME THE THREAT OF THE OTTOMAN TURKS WHO HAD POURED INTO THE BALKANS.

Constantinople remained under threat, however, and despite some unsuccessful campaigns to relieve pressure on this iconic city, the unthinkable happened when Constantinople fell to the Ottoman Turks, led by Sultan Mehmed II, on 6 April 1453, after a 53-day siege. Mehmed subsequently campaigned west, explicitly stating Rome as an objective, but this ambition was quashed with Mehmed's death on 3 May 1481.

Above: The Ottoman army under Mehmed II, who was just 21 at the time, captured Constantinople in May 1453, signalling the final end of the Byzantine Empire.

CONCLUSION

Crusading in its original sense – a military-religious act of pilgrimage – died out during the sixteenth century. There were vestiges of the crusading spirit left, such as the formations of Holy Leagues to fight wars ostensibly under a Christian banner; a key example of this is the naval battle of Lepanto on 7 October 1571 between a Holy League led by Venice and Spain and the Ottoman Turks. Yet the major contextual event that ended the Crusades was the rise of Protestantism in Europe, which broke the hold the Catholic Church had over much of the continent, and held the very concept of the Crusade under suspicion.

Although the act of crusading has now long gone, the language of the Crusades has been more enduring. During the world wars, for example, it was standard practice to declare that God was on your side, even though the other side was declaring exactly the same thing. Rising secularism in Europe means that the return to faith-framed militarism is unlikely, but given the tensions that remain between the West and the Middle East, we should always be mindful of the Crusades as resonant lessons from history.

FURTHER READING

Asbridge, Thomas, *The Crusades: The War for the Holy Land* (London, Simon & Schuster, 2010)

Brundage, James, *The Crusades: A Documentary History* (Milwaukee, WI, Marquette University Press, 1962)

Byrom, Jamie and Michael Riley, *The Crusades* (London, Hodder, 2013)

Ellenblum, Ronnie, *Crusader Castles and Modern Histories* (Cambridge, Cambridge University Press, 2009)

Hindley, Geoffrey, *Saladin: Hero of Islam* (Bradford, Pen & Sword, 2010)

Hindley, Geoffrey, *The Crusades: Islam and Christianity in the Struggle for World Supremacy* (London, Robinson, 2004)

Jean de Joinville, *The Memoirs of the Lord of Joinville: A New English Version*, trans. by Ethel Wedgwood (New York, E.P. Dutton and Co. 1906)

Jones, Dan, *The Templars: The Rise and Fall of God's Holy Warriors* (London, Head of Zeus, 2018)

King, Edwin James, *The Knights Hospitallers in the Holy Land* (London, Methuen, 1931)

Nicolle, David, *Crusader Castles in the Holy Land: An Illustrated History of the Crusader Fortifications of the Middle East and Mediterranean* (Oxford, Osprey, 2010)

Nicolle, David, *The First Crusade 1096–99: Conquest of the Holy Land* (Oxford, Osprey, 2003)

Nicolle, David, *The Second Crusade 1148: Disaster outside Damascus* (Oxford, Osprey, 2008)

Nicolle, David, *The Third Crusade 1191: Richard the Lionheart, Saladin and Struggle for Jerusalem* (Oxford, Osprey, 2005)

Nicolle, David, *The Fourth Crusade 1202–04: The Betrayal of Byzantium* (Oxford, Osprey, 2011)

Peters, Edward (ed.), *The First Crusade: the Chronicle of Fulcher of Chartres and Other Source Materials* (Philadelphia, PA, University of Pennsylvania Press 1998)

Stone, Edward N. (ed.) *Three Old French Chronicles of the Crusades* (Seattle, University of Washington, 1939)

Thatcher, Oliver J., and Edgar Holmes McNeal (eds), *A Source Book for Medieval History* (New York, Scribners, 1905)

Tyerman, Christopher, *God's War: A New History of the Crusades* (London, Penguin, 2007)

Tyerman, Christopher, *How to Plan a Crusade* (London, Penguin, 2015)

Williams, Hywel, *The Age of Chivalry: Culture and Power in Medieval Europe 950–1450* (London, Quercus, 2011)

Wise, Terence, *Armies of the Crusades* (Oxford, Osprey, 1978)

INDEX

Page numbers in **bold** refer to illustration captions.

PICTURE CREDITS

Alamy: 9 (Photo 12), 11 (BibleLandPictures.com), 13 (Ian Dagnall), 16 (BLM Collection), 21 (Westend61/ Martin Siepman), 26 (Photo 12), 27 (Archivart), 31 (Lanmas), 33 (Science History Images), 35 (The Granger Collection), 37 (Falkensteinfoto), 38 (Chronicle), 41 (Interfoto), 43 (Science History Images), 46 (Niday Picture Library), 51 (Art Heritage), 54 (Interfoto), 55 (Chronicle), 59 (Lanmas), 61 (Science History Images), 65 (Art Heritage), 72 (Nir Alon), 73 (Historical Image Collection by Bildagentur-online), 74 (Interfoto), 77 (imageBROKER), 79 (Interfoto), 80 (age fotostock), 82 (Historical Image Collection by Bildagentur-online), 83 (Prisma Archivo), 85 (Classic Image), 87 (bilwissedition Ltd & Co.KG), 89 (ASP Religion), 90 (Prisma Archivo), 96 (Falkensteinfoto), 99 (Artepics), 100 (Interfoto), 101 (imageBROKER), 103 (classic image), 105 (stock montage, Inc), 106 (Chronicle), 108 (Artokoloro Quint Lox Limited), 118 (oldtime), 130 (Pictorial Press Ltd), 131 (photo 12), 132 (GL Archive), 134 (De Luan), 137 (Science History Images), 142 (Classic Image), 143 (Science History Images), 145 (Classic Image), 148 (The Picture Art Collection), 150 (Niday Picture Library), 151 (Hirarchivum Press), 152 (Falkensteinfoto), 155 (Art Collection), 168 (riccardo Moncioli), 175 (Historical Image Collection by Bildagentur-online), 176 (Yolanda Perera Sanchez), 178 (SuperStock), 179 (Niday Picture Library), 181 & 185 (Chronicle), 186 top (The History Collection), 194 (SuperStock), 195 & 196 (Falkensteinfoto), 197 & 198 (Science History Images), 199 (Chronicle), 201 (Interfoto), 202 (The History Collection), 203 (Classic Image), 206 (Science History Images), 209 (Pictorial Press Ltd), 210 (Prisma Archivo), 213 (Yolanda Perera Sanchez), 219 (imageBROKER)

Alamy/Granger Historical Picture Research: 6, 40, 44, 53, 153, 160, 188, 205

Alamy/ Heritage Image Partnership Ltd: 20, 36, 62, 66, 68, 71, 94, 102, 119, 122, 139, 158 & 159, 172, 216

Alamy/World History Archive: 8, 17, 24, 28, 88, 98, 110, 190/ 191 & 192

Amber Books/Art-Tech: 48/49, 75, 123, 141 top & bottom, 144, 161 all, 189, 214

Bridgeman Images: 10 (Biblioteque Nationale, Paris, France), 29 & 30 (Look & Learn), 34 (DeAgostini/A. Dagli Orti), 39 (Stapleton Collection), 50 (British Library Board), 56 (DeAgostini/F.Gallino), 60 (Biblioteque Nationale, Paris, France), 67 (Biblioteque Nationale, Paris, France), 86 (Stapleton Collection), 91 (Private Collection), 97 (Bridgeman), 113 (British Library Board), 115 (Biblioteque Nationale, Paris, France), 121 (Chateau de Versailles), 124 (G Dagli Orti), 138 (Bridgeman), 147 (Look & Learn), 156 (DeAgostini/G.Dagli Orti), 167 (Biblioteque Nationale, Paris, France), 182 (Patrice Cartier), 204 (Louvre)

Dreamstime: 19 (Przemyslaw Borkowski), 22 (Antonella865), 93 (Didewide), 116 (Jorisvo), 133 (Photographieundmehr), 135 (Georgios Kollidas), 170 (Juan Moyano), 186/187 bottom (Mariusz Burcz)

Getty Images: 14 (ZU-09), 70 (Josse/Leemage), 120 (Heritage Images), 126 (DeAgostini/G Dagli Orti), 128 & 164 (Josse/Leemage), 166 (Werner Forman)

Shutterstock: 92 (Alaa AbuMadi)